Interactive Writing: A Small Practice With Big Results, PreK–5

Kate Roth & Joan Dabrowski

Stenhouse Publishers
www.stenhouse.com

International Literacy Association
www.literacyworldwide.org

Library of Congress Cataloging-in-Publication Data
[To come]

Cover Design, Martha Drury; Photographs, Kate Roth and Joan Dabrowski
Author Photographs by Andrea Topalian and Kara Billhardt

Manufactured in the United States of America

22 21 20 19 18 17 16   9 8 7 6 5 4 3 2 1

For our parents

CONTENTS

ABOUT THE AUTHORS

Kate Roth has been a classroom teacher, Reading Recovery teacher, researcher, and literacy coach in the United States and abroad. Much of her work has focused on the interactive writing method and supporting teachers in their effort to implement it. Kate has also published 20 books for children on how to write as part of the Language Arts Explorer Junior series. She earned a master's degree at Columbia University, Teachers College, and her doctorate of education in language and literacy at the Harvard Graduate School of Education.

Joan Dabrowski is a literacy consultant and curriculum writer who works across the country with teachers and literacy coaches. In addition, she works extensively with school and district leaders to develop and refine their literacy and leadership practices. She has taught grades K–2 and 4–5 and has been a district literacy coach and administrator. She earned a master's degree at the Harvard Graduate School of Education and a doctorate of education in K–12 school leadership at Vanderbilt University, Peabody College.

ACKNOWLEDGMENTS

Our professional lives are enriched by many who guide us in essential ways.

This book would not be possible without the thoughtful work of dedicated teachers who brought interactive writing to life in their classrooms. Their willingness to work and think with us about the method allowed us to capture important details, try out new features, refine our ideas, broaden our perspective, and solidify the guidance we offer in this book. Their commitment to this project is reflected in many of the writing samples included in the chapters and in many of the suggestions we offer around implementation. Our thanks to Pinnecko Artise, Melissa Brooks, Paige Brown, Roxanne DeStefano, Jeff Ginter, Emily Gold, Lisa Hoy, JoAnn Jones, Christy Klump, Heather Knight, Atara Leamon, Mollie McAllister, Heather McIsaac, Laurie Myrick, Brendan Newman, Cristina Pelaez, Keri Purple, Michelle Starks, Cassandra Tang, Darlene Wallace, and Krystle Winter.

We also acknowledge the school leaders who supported this project by welcoming us into their buildings, scheduling our visits, or arranging times for us to meet with teachers. Their literacy leadership efforts did not go unnoticed. Our thanks to Daniel Eschtruth, Roxanne Forr, Melanie Knudsen, and Andrew Powell.

From the very beginning, we knew that having trusted colleagues read our early article and chapter drafts would bring important insights and perspectives. They did not let us down as they asked important questions, offered concrete suggestions, and pushed our thinking. Their honest and thoughtful feedback makes the final version of this book more complete. We acknowledge these thought partners and are grateful for their expertise. Our thanks to Brett Berkman, Jon Eckert, Jennifer Friedman, Rebecca Glick, Natalie Grey, Martha Heller-Winokur, Toni Jolley, Karen King, Kim Marshall, Laurie Myrick, Jon Saphier, and Jeff Winokur.

We are indebted to the outstanding educators who taught us and who continue to inform our work. Our thanks especially to OJ Burns, Irene Fountas, Linda Garbus, Nonie Lesaux, Joseph Murphy, Gay Su Pinnell, Amy Schwartz, and Catherine Snow.

Writing this book was a journey filled with twists, turns, and many "and then" stories. We are grateful for the two publishing teams who shepherded us through the process. At International Literacy Association (ILA), our thanks to Shannon Fortner, Becky Fetterolf, and Christina Lambert for the many calls and emails that turned our ideas into a manuscript. At Stenhouse, we acknowledge the creative work of Jay Kilburn, Chris Downey, Zsofia McMullin, Chuck Lerch, and Martha Drury. Most importantly, our gratitude to the always thoughtful and responsive Tori Bachman who believed in our work from the very beginning and enthusiastically brought this book to the finish line!

We are anchored by our families. Their love has always been boundless and unconditional, and for that we are most grateful.

To our parents, Richard and Nan, Stan and Kay: Thank you for your help -- as parents and as grandparents -- as this project spilled into many of our weekends and vacations. Please know that we all feel well cared for when you are with us.

To our children, Annabel, Andrew, and Alexandria, Lindy and Collins: As we wrote this book, you represented our living and breathing K-8 writing continuum and served as a powerful reminder of what it means to be a student writer in the 21st century. We are continually inspired by you! Thank you for enriching our lives. The ball games, swim meets, concerts, recitals, beach days, school events, and many many snow days together this past winter kept our work in check and our lives grounded.

And to our husbands, Erik and Stephen: Thank you for your love and encouragement. Your support has been unwavering. The many SMALL things you do yield BIG results for us.

Interactive Writing: A *Small* Practice With *Big* Results

Interactive writing is a powerful approach to writing instruction. Initially designed to support emergent writers, it has been used recently in upper elementary classrooms with great success. When done on a regular basis, interactive writing has the potential to improve students' independent writing. The method is systematic and follows a predictable routine but is far from a teacher-scripted approach. Rather, it harnesses the natural interactions you have with students as they compose a writing piece. In this book, we call it a *small* practice with *big* results.

By *small*, we mean that interactive writing is manageable. It is a singular and straightforward practice that pulls your language and literacy program together around a shared piece of writing. Interactive writing stands alone as a method for you to master while simultaneously complementing your other methods of instruction. It is designed to be part of a rich and balanced program of literacy instruction.

The potential results are *big* both for students *and* for you. Interactive writing is, at its heart, a collaborative and *interactive* experience. As you work to understand this approach to teaching, which delves deep into the writing process, you and your students inevitably have rich conversations about writing. The method has been shown to improve students' independent writing, which is the ultimate goal (Roth & Guinee, 2011).

Along the way, *you* will also work through the many facets and components of writing in small steps. Immersing ourselves in this method has crystallized our understanding of the qualities of good writing and instruction. We hope that as you read this book and try out interactive writing in your classroom, you will experience the same "aha" moments that we have.

Our Story

Kate: My Journey to This Book

The story of this book begins more than 20 years ago when I was a new teacher. I was trying different methods of instruction to help my first graders learn to read and write. At that time, Irene Fountas was the literacy coordinator in my school. She was advocating that teachers incorporate a relatively new method called interactive writing.

Together Irene and I taught interactive writing lessons in my classroom, and I was hooked from the beginning. I loved the energy of the lessons, the way I was pulling together my entire literacy curriculum in every interactive writing session, the opportunity to reach so many students at different levels while creating a community of writers, and the rich and authentic products we created.

Throughout the next several years, I implemented interactive writing on a daily basis with my primary-grade students in both urban and suburban classrooms. It became one of the core teaching practices in my class. During this time, I also trained as a Reading Recovery teacher. The more I learned about students' literacy development and how assessment informs good instruction, the more I was convinced of the power of this practice to help improve students' independent writing.

When I pursued my doctorate in language and literacy, my research focused on interactive writing in the primary grades. I was thrilled, although not surprised, that my research findings confirmed my classroom experience: Interactive writing is a powerful method for improving students' independent writing. My studies offer five main conclusions about the effectiveness of interactive writing (Roth, 2009; Roth & Guinee, 2011):

1. *During interactive writing sessions, teachers are able to address a wide range of concepts and strategies about writing.* Lessons regularly address concepts related to ideas, organization, word choice, sentence fluency, voice, conventions of print, spelling, and handwriting. These findings confirm results from a study by Brotherton and Williams (2002) indicating that interactive writing can provide "many opportunities to teach critical and fundamental literacy concepts" (p. 8).

2. *Students who participate in interactive writing show growth on multiple measures of independent writing.* Students are able to transfer the many skills and strategies addressed in each lesson.

3. *Students at all levels of literacy can benefit from interactive writing instruction.* Although not all students progress in all areas simultaneously, interactive writing is an effective way to differentiate instruction within a whole-class lesson.

4. *Interactive writing is relatively easy to implement in that it is cost- and time-effective.* Minimal materials are needed, and the lessons are relatively short in duration.

5. *Interactive writing can be a valuable component in a comprehensive early literacy program.* Although it is a rich and effective method, it is not a method that is meant to be used in isolation. The approach is designed to be a valuable part of a balanced early literacy framework that offers myriad opportunities for teacher instruction, shared literacy experiences, and independent problem solving within a literacy-rich classroom (Button, Johnson, & Furgerson, 1996). Students need additional teacher instruction and time to write independently and practice what they are learning.

These powerful findings fueled my decision to refine and expand my understandings of interactive writing through additional action research and coaching both abroad and in the United States. At that time, I was living in Shanghai, China, and had an opportunity to work with teachers in grades PreK–4 as part of a yearlong intensive study of interactive writing. As part of this experience, teachers kept detailed logs of their regular implementation of the method, and I coached them each week in their classroom. As I moved through the year with this cohort of teachers, I realized quickly that interactive writing made sense for students as young as prekindergarten as well as for upper-grade writers. At this point, I invited my longtime colleague and friend to join me on this journey. Let's back up for a moment to get a sense of how of this partnership evolved.

Joan: My Journey to This Book

My entry into this book project was indeed much later than Kate's. Yet our first *connection* came more than 15 years ago when we met as teachers at the Mather School in Boston, Massachusetts. Our principal, Kim Marshall (a champion of instructional leadership), encouraged us every day to use the best instructional methods available to support our students. Kim's steadfast commitment to instruction came hand in hand with resources, professional development opportunities, and weekly grade-level planning meetings.

Despite these opportunities, Kate and I saw each other rarely during our two-year overlap at Mather. While she implemented interactive writing daily with her first graders on the lower level of the building, I taught writing as best as I knew how to my fourth and fifth graders three floors above her. I modeled my own writing, scribed for my students, and shared with them texts written by authors. I dabbled in the six traits and frequently analyzed my students' writing, seeking answers for where to go next. Although all of these methods helped my students, I knew that they needed more explicit guidance.

As my interest in literacy and leadership grew, I moved into coaching positions at both the school and district levels in Cambridge, Massachusetts.

In these roles, I had the opportunity to write curriculum, facilitate district-wide scoring of writing assignments, and support many teachers in grades 3–5. At the same time, I pursued my doctoral degree in school leadership and administration, keeping a close eye on the world of literacy.

Upon graduation, I moved into different consulting and literacy leadership roles, including director of literacy for the Boston Public Schools. Each of these experiences offered me a wider view of schools and classrooms. As I worked with school leaders and observed teachers across the United States, I recognized a common challenge: Writing instruction was given neither the time nor the attention it needed. Many teachers were looking for ways to develop their student writers and were eager for concrete guidance on *how* to do so efficiently and effectively.

As Kate and I pursued our different paths, we stayed in contact frequently. We shared our professional stories with each other and sought the other's advice for projects we pursued. In the spring of 2012, we began talking more and more about writing instruction. At that time, Kate was living in Shanghai, and I was living in Hawaii. Kate had plans to introduce interactive writing to a group of upper-grades teachers and wondered what I thought about this idea. I needed to know more, so I read Kate's research enthusiastically. Over the next year, she and I kept in touch about her experiences with the upper grades. Hearing about what she was learning with and from teachers was exciting; now *I* was hooked!

Kate: Our Collaboration

In the spring of 2013, I asked Joan to join me on this project. I knew that our combined enthusiasm and unique perspectives would strengthen the work that I had begun. Using my yearlong study in international schools in China as a foundation, we mapped out how interactive writing evolves as it moves up through the grades, and we identified important factors and patterns that make the approach valuable from PreK–5. At the same time, we read and considered what others were saying on the topic (e.g., Fisher & Frey, 2007b; Fisher & Frey, 2013; Mermelstein, 2013; Wall, 2008; Williams, Sherry, Robinson, & Hungler, 2012). We also widened the approach to embrace the various forms of technology that support its implementation. From interactive whiteboards to document cameras and laptops, we harnessed what it means to use this method in a 21st-century classroom.

Our most recent findings demonstrate that interactive writing is a powerful practice that extends easily through fifth grade (Roth & Dabrowski, 2014). The underlying theory of the method in addition to the principles of effective teaching support the success of this method for all PreK–5 writers. Interactive writing helps young children make progress in their writing by inviting them to participate, *with support*, in the act of writing (McCarrier, Pinnell, & Fountas, 2000). This makes sense for *all* developing writers.

Over the past two years, we have partnered with additional teachers in grades 3–5 in order to learn more. We have taught interactive writing lessons together with them, planned with them, and discussed the many nuances of how this method works (or does not work) at particular moments across the school year. We looked closely at student writing and noticed the places where interactive writing influenced their work positively. We thought about how the method changes for older writers and how the curriculum influences the frequency and duration of the lessons.

The response of the teachers and students in the upper elementary grades has been energizing and affirming! We truly enjoy supporting teachers in *all* elementary grades as they take on this practice in their own classrooms. And so we embarked on this book-writing adventure together to share our findings and enthusiasm about interactive writing with teachers both near and far.

Another Book About Writing?! Why?

Over the past decade, much has been written about the writing crisis in the United States and the real-life harm this causes for so many (e.g., Graham & Harris, 2014; Graham, Harris, & Hebert, 2011; Graham & Hebert, 2010; Graham & Perin, 2007b; Lee, Grigg, & Donahue, 2007; National Commission on Writing in America's Schools and Colleges, 2003; Yancey, 2009). We hear time and again that many students are not prepared adequately to write well (National Center for Education Statistics, 2012). Thus, their opportunities for future success and economic stability are compromised.

We also hear that writing instruction receives less attention each day than other interests and curricular priorities, including reading and math (Gilbert & Graham, 2010; Rideout, Foehr, & Roberts, 2010; Shanahan, 2014). We know that teaching students how to write is a highly complex task that requires both content knowledge and pedagogical skill (Bromley, 2011; Graham & Harris, 2013). Suffice it to say that writing matters—a lot! It matters for school, home, and life. It matters for personal, social, academic, and economic reasons. The importance of developing young people's writing skills cannot be overstated.

Fortunately, there is widespread agreement that writing instruction must be pushed to the forefront of our educational agenda (e.g., Ganske, 2014; Graham & Harris, 2013; Graham & Perin, 2007b; Jago, 2014). We know that in order to develop writing skills commensurate with literacy standards, children must begin their foundation for writing in the primary grades, especially given that writing performance is related strongly to their later success (Graham & Harris, 2013; Juel, 1988; Morrow, Tracey, & Del Nero, 2011).

Recent publications have identified key elements of effective writing instruction and have called out the types of writing that students must know and understand (Bromley, 2011; Ganske, 2014; Graham, MacArthur, & Fitzgerald, 2013). New standards expect students to engage in the writing process and to write routinely. They also require students to write concisely, deeply, and, therefore, with more authority (National Governors Association Center for Best Practices & Council of Chief State School Officers, 2010).

For us, this is where interactive writing enters the conversation. The case has been made that we must do a better job of teaching students to write. We also have clear guidance on both the kinds of writing that students must experience and the qualities of good writing (Culham, 2003; Culham, 2005; Spandel, 2013). It is time for us to revisit and refine the best *teaching* practices to answer the question of *how* to teach writing. We believe that teachers play an *indispensable* role in a child's process of learning to write, and thus high-quality instruction is crucial to improving writing outcomes.

Interactive writing is an instructionally rich teaching practice linked to stronger independent writing. It is systematic (though not scripted!) and follows a predictable routine. The explicitness and efficiency of interactive writing make it a particularly effective teaching practice that can support both emergent and fluent writers. We want you to know and understand this method so that you can add it to your repertoire of writing instruction. As we said in the opening paragraph, interactive writing is a small, manageable practice that, when done well, yields big results for students (and you!).

Navigating the Book

This book is designed as a how-to. As you will see, we unpack the interactive writing method step by step. Our ultimate hope is that when you finish the final chapter, you will know and understand the method well enough to try it out for yourself. With that goal in mind, we have organized this book into three sections. Section One provides an overview of the method and lays out how it fits into a comprehensive literacy framework. Section Two zooms in on each step of the lesson sequence. Section Three suggests concrete ways to launch interactive writing in your classroom and identifies important universal principles that hold for interactive writing in every grade.

Section One: An Overview of Interactive Writing

We begin Chapter 1 with our definition of interactive writing. We then share authentic interactive writing pieces composed by *real* teachers with *real* students in grades PreK–5. These samples show a diverse gradient of text in addition to writing across many genres. As you read and analyze the writing samples, we highlight the teaching and learning that occurred within each of these pieces. Through these annotated details, we make our introductory case for the instructional value of this method: *Using interactive writing regularly with your students will help them become better independent writers*.

In Chapter 2, we list and define the basic sequence of an interactive writing lesson. We emphasize that the sequence is predictable and each step holds important value. The second part of this chapter helps you understand where and how interactive writing fits within your literacy framework. We share how interactive writing connects with the writing process and the gradual release of responsibility model. We note that interactive writing is *not* meant to be an exclusive practice. Rather, we encourage you to include a range of writing practices to support your students. Further, we highlight how interactive writing integrates with your broader language and literacy program as it simultaneously supports children's oral language and reading development.

Section Two: Working Through Each Part of an Interactive Writing Lesson

Chapter 3 is the first in a series of six chapters that explores in detail a step within the lesson. In this chapter, we discuss experience and why it matters in interactive writing. Specifically, we focus on the importance of a *shared* classroom experience and emphasize the benefits this brings when you move into the Compose phase of a lesson. We provide examples of possible classroom experiences that work well for interactive writing.

Chapter 4 addresses the Prewrite portion of an interactive writing lesson. Here, we look closely at how you determine the purpose the writing holds, the best form the writing should take, and the audience who will read it. We then discuss how Prewrite begins to formalize as writers move up through the grades.

Chapter 5 and Chapter 6 (the longest chapters of the book!) describe the heart of the interactive writing method: Compose and Share the Pen. In Chapter 5, we dive deeply into Compose, the time when you and your students work together to negotiate the precise words you will write. Together you think through the ideas emphasized and the organization in which they are presented. You work collaboratively with your students to choose each word or phrase to combine them in a sentence with the right voice and structure for the genre. The emphasis is on how to help your students with the *craft* of writing.

In Chapter 6, we describe the innovative writing technique unique to interactive writing called Share the Pen. During Share the Pen, you and your students take turns with the pen or marker to write the text that was crafted during Compose. The teaching emphasis during this phase of the lesson shifts to writing *conventions*. Conventions matter a lot! And, conventions can be a gatekeeper for student writers trying to meet the ever-demanding grade-level standards and expectations. This chapter also includes important modifications for what it means to "write" in the 21st century. For older and more fluent writers, Share the Pen becomes Share the Keyboard, and the teaching emphasis around conventions widens to include real-time revisions (e.g., spell-check, cut and paste), keyboarding, and technology features (e.g., font, layout, color).

In Chapter 7 and Chapter 8, we look closely at Review and Extend, the final steps that bring closure to an interactive writing lesson. During Review, you and your students interact with the finished writing piece in order to reinforce the important writing skills that were taught during Compose and Share the Pen. Then, you summarize these important teaching points and remind students to apply these same principles to their independent writing. There are interesting and creative ways to engage students during Review. We provide many examples for leading students through a thoughtful, but quick, Review.

In Chapter 8, we discuss the many ways you can extend the completed interactive writing piece. By this point, you and your students will have invested a great amount of time and effort into a collaborative piece of writing. Thus, it is the perfect piece to use for further teaching and application. In this chapter, we show and describe a variety of extensions and point out how these extensions support students' overall literacy development. You will learn how Extend motivates your student writers, pulls together the many pieces of your literacy curriculum, and supports your students' independent writing.

Section Three: Getting Started With Interactive Writing

Chapter 9 suggests strategic ways to prepare for interactive writing in your classroom. We highlight eight points that address topics such as classroom arrangement, materials, routines, and teacher planning. Taken together, these points will support you as you launch this method and make it your own. Chapter 10 pulls all of the pieces of the practice together. We share interactive writing samples from each grade level and summarize how the steps together form a cohesive and comprehensive lesson. Finally, we share five universal principles for interactive writing for PreK–5.

A Book for Grades PreK–5

From the onset, we were committed to writing a book that would speak to teachers in grades PreK–5, as we firmly believe this method holds important value across *all* elementary grades. That said, we wanted to simultaneously honor the important developmental differences and needs that exist for our emergent, developing, and fluent writers. These developmental differences cannot always be sorted neatly into the grade levels we teach. For example, it is not uncommon to have an emergent writer in second or third grade.

As we wrote each chapter, whenever possible, we wanted to include an image or table to support your understanding. These represent quick reads of important points along the way. We envision them as helpful "one-pagers" for you to use as you plan for interactive writing. However, as we constructed the images throughout the book, we sometimes found ourselves stuck when deciding which grade level to include.

In the end, we agreed that grade 2 was, indeed, an important year of transition. The beginning of second grade may feel quite simple and concrete in terms of students' writing. But as the year unfolds, you may see second-grade writing that is both longer and more sophisticated. So, as you will see, many of our images are organized as PreK–2 and grades 2–5. This represents our best approximations of where students typically may be in relation to their writing development and how the second-grade year can find itself in both a primary- and upper-grade place depending upon the students and time of year.

A key guiding principle for us is that interactive writing works best when you consider the needs of *your* students first. We encourage you to look above and below your grade level when you use these visuals and, for that matter, whenever you plan for interactive writing. This wider lens ensures that you are supporting and advancing the diverse needs of your student writers.

Voices From the Classroom

Throughout the book, you will notice quotations in the margins. We call these "What Teachers Are Saying." The quotes capture what teachers and literacy coaches across all grade levels PreK–5 believe about interactive writing. Their voices represent the many with whom we have worked and coached around this method. Through their words, you get a sense of how they and their students have benefited from this approach. You also hear how they teach through each phase of the lesson and how they make adjustments as they go. Hearing this genuine perspective is empowering.

In the same spirit, we have included excerpts from interactive writing lessons in grades PreK–5. We call these excerpts "Listen in on a Lesson." As you "listen in," you will notice how the method comes alive in classrooms as teachers move through the lesson sequence. You will learn how teachers balance the planned moments while honoring the spontaneous teaching opportunities that arise.

Different Paths for Different Readers

Although our initial vision of the book was to organize a sequential collection of chapters that could be read from start to finish, we anticipate that different readers will bring unique experiences and understandings to this text. These perspectives may influence how you navigate the book. For the *beginning teacher* who may be new to the teaching profession and to the method itself, we encourage you to move through the book as we have laid it out. For the *seasoned teacher* who has been using other types of writing approaches (e.g., writers' workshop, modeled writing, shared writing), looking closely at Chapter 2 to discover how interactive writing is different and holds a unique place within the gradual release of responsibility model may be helpful.

For the *K–2 teacher who has been using interactive writing for many years*, we invite you to move through the chapters with an eye toward the headings and subheadings that provide updated and refined nuances. For example, the guidance we provide around teaching language during Compose and Share the Pen may be new for you. We also suggest you explore how technology can be integrated.

For the *literacy coach*, seeing the PreK–5 continuum of the method will be important for you. Your teachers will have a range of needs and will teach a range of students. Knowing how the method changes as it moves up the grades will be a priority. You may also appreciate each chapter's guiding questions, the "Listen in on a Lesson" sections, and the planning templates, which can inform teacher planning and development sessions.

We also honor that each reader may need or want different points addressed at particular moments in his or her learning. For example, if you want to see this practice in its entirety right away, then the place to begin is in Chapter 1. However, if your preference is to first understand how the method is sequenced and to know where it fits within a comprehensive literacy framework, start with Chapter 2. If classroom logistics are preventing you from fully understanding how the method might flow, move into Chapter 9, where we highlight important planning and preparation points. For *all* readers, we hope the many tables and images support your visual learning and bring the method alive for you.

Final Thoughts

This book is our invitation to consider (or reconsider) interactive writing as a *small* writing practice that yields *big* results. Our own journeys to this book were filled with twists and turns, but we have landed here together on solid ground. Your entry into this book will be unique as well. Regardless of how you arrived, we welcome you and encourage you to jump in and start reading with your eyes wide open! We trust that this book has something for you. Enjoy!

An Overview
of Interactive Writing

CHAPTER 1

A First Look at Interactive Writing

Discover the power of interactive writing! This chapter introduces the method by analyzing finished pieces from prekindergarten through fifth grade (PreK–5). As we move through each piece, we uncover the hidden teaching processes within.

Good teaching happens when we consider the end goals for students. Before a lesson begins, you think about your student writers: who they are, what they need next in their writing development, and how you will get them there. It is with that same spirit that we jump into the exploration of interactive writing. We have thought a lot about *your* needs as writing *teachers* and how best to support your writing *instruction*. And so we begin with our quick definition of the interactive writing method, followed by snapshots of finished interactive writing pieces. These pieces may spark your interest, prompt your thinking, and cause you to ask questions. We invite you to consider the power and possibilities of interactive writing.

Interactive Writing: Quick Definition

Interactive writing is a dynamic instructional method during which the teacher serves as the expert writer for her students as they work together to construct a meaningful text while simultaneously discussing the details of the writing process. Together, they plan, compose, and review text in a variety of genres. The "interactive" piece involves group collaboration in planning and composing the writing through guided conversation and a unique "sharing the pen" technique where students do the actual writing.

Throughout interactive writing, there are frequent opportunities to differentiate instruction in order to meet individual student needs. For example, the teacher selectively chooses how each student will participate in the lesson. This decision is informed

WHAT TEACHERS ARE SAYING

I like that interactive writing explicitly teaches and models all aspects of writing in one short, daily minilesson. We are able to cover so much in such a short amount of time.

—Krystle (PreK)

by data—what the teacher already knows about her writers. Additionally, she negotiates which teaching points to emphasize based on the instructional value for her students at that given point in time.

A Picture Is Worth a Thousand Words: Part One

Finished pieces of interactive writing help us see this definition more clearly. They are a window into the process in which the class engaged. The following seven pieces are grade-level samples produced during interactive writing lessons in each grade, PreK through 5. Let's begin by looking at all seven pieces together before we focus on each one individually.

Use the following three prompts to guide you:

1. What elements of the writing **craft** do you notice? (Focus on ideas, organization, language and sentence structure, word choice, and voice.)
2. What do you notice about writing **conventions**? (Focus on concepts of print, text layout, grammar, capitalization, punctuation, spelling, and handwriting.)
3. What might the teacher be working on with these student writers?

Use this QR code or the URL below to access full-color student samples at www.stenhouse.com/ interactivewritingbook

PreK Sample

Kindergarten Sample

Grade 1 Sample

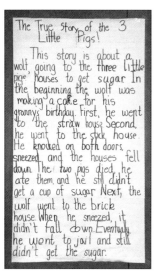

Grade 2 Sample

Panning is really popular in the gold fields because it is cheap, pans are not easy to find, they are simple to use and anyone can do it. To pan, you will need the following things: a pan, gravel, dirt, a shovel, a pick-axe, a hoe and a container for your gold. First, use the hoe, pick-axe, and shovel to gather and collect the dirt. Then, take the dirt, put it in the pan and take it near the river. Dip the pan in the river and shake the pan in a swaying side-to-side motion. Next, take the pan out of the river. After that, if you have gold in your pan it should be heavier than the dirt and sink to the bottom. If there is gold in your pan, secretly put it in your pocket or container. Finally, you can take it to the bank and exchange it for lots and lots of money!

Grade 3 Sample

In the book *Where the Mountain Meets the Moon* by Grace Lin, Ma is an important character who changes throughout the story. In the beginning, Ma is depressed. For example, she always gives a heavy sigh when Ba tells his stories.

In the middle of the story, Ma is becoming less depressed and more hopeful. An example of this is when Ba tells the story of The Paper of Happiness. Ma doesn't sigh, instead she listens to his story.

By the end of the story, Ma seemed joyful, grateful, and wiser. In Chapter 44 when Ma told her story she began to realize that she had been ungrateful and selfish by not being thankful for what she had like their food, home, family and Ba's stories.

Grade 4 Sample

The Water Cycle

Evaporation is when the sun's heat energy transforms liquid water into water vapor. Evaporation occurs in all bodies of water like lakes, rivers, oceans, and ponds. Next, water vapor rises into the sky and it cools, changing back into liquid form. The water vapor condenses to form clouds. Gravity pulls rain, snow, sleet, and hail back to Earth's surface in a process called precipitation. The sun is always shining; therefore, the Water Cycle is continuously moving and purifying our water.

Grade 5 Sample

A First Look at the Product: Key Characteristics of Interactive Writing Pieces

Taken as a group, the products have important commonalities that help us understand this method of instruction. They also illustrate how you make adjustments as writers mature and change over time. Here's what we notice when we look at all seven pieces together:

- Students write about a range of authentic experiences. The experiences are familiar to every student in the class (i.e., field trip to the zoo, class party, science unit on solids and liquids, a class read-aloud, social studies unit on the Gold Rush, a novel that was read together, and science unit on the water cycle).

- There are opportunities to teach about the craft and conventions of writing in every piece.

- The writing is well structured; it is easy to follow the piece from beginning to end.

- There are a variety of writing forms; each piece has a different authentic purpose (i.e., to retell an event, to say thank you, to record important ideas in science, to summarize a favorite book, to explain a concept in social studies, to describe a character, and to summarize a scientific process).

- Words are selected thoughtfully to enhance meaning and to stretch student vocabulary.

- A range of sentences is included that promotes the flow of interesting and specific language; sentences become increasingly complex as the writers develop.

WHAT TEACHERS ARE SAYING

I love all that it incorporates into one lesson. Concepts of print, handwriting, word study, and sentence structure can all be taught in one lesson. —Heather K. (Kindergarten)

- Spelling is conventional.
- Grammar and punctuation are standard.
- Layout issues have been considered:
  - Handwriting is neat; upper- and lowercase letters are formed accurately and proportionately.
  - The pieces are written with black marker on sentence strips or on lined paper with letters that are relatively uniform and with clear spacing between words.
  - The pieces in grades 3, 4, and 5 are typed using conventional layout and fonts.
  - Editing occurs throughout; errors are corrected in the moment using white tape or spell-check tools.
  - Illustrations enhance the text; the pictures take many forms (e.g., painting, photographs, drawings).
- Each piece is written at a text level that is meant for students in that grade to reread.

A Closer Look Grade by Grade: Beginning to Understand the Process

There are significant consistencies in the process and products created during interactive writing at all grade levels. However, let's now look closely at each writing sample by itself. This analysis helps you understand a bit more about the teaching and learning that happened in each lesson and shows how instruction adjusts over time as readers and writers become more fluent.

Prekindergarten (PreK)

The PreK writing piece reminds us that our youngest students have much to say and write about their learning. In this sample, we see an excerpt from a multiple-page book that retells the story of a field trip to the zoo. Because the trip was a shared experience, all students engaged with the ideas and content of the

Retell of a Field Trip (PreK)

writing. This engagement is essential, as the most basic connections between reading, writing, and speaking are new to young children.

Students' vocabulary expanded as they discussed words such as *giraffe*, *tiger*, *rhinoceros*, and *zebra*. The phrase "We saw a..." is reinforced on every page of this book, as it is repeated intentionally for each animal observed on the trip. The benefit of the repetitive text allows for frequent rereading as well as an opportunity to teach three high-frequency words that will show up in students' independent writing in the weeks that follow.

Notice that the writing contains four words that are spaced apart intentionally by cutting the sentence strip. Notice also that the sentence begins with a capital letter and ends with a period. There is considerable focus on concepts about print for this grade; directionality and the idea of letters versus words versus sentences are highlighted. The individual letters in each word were written by different students along with help from the teacher. Students wrote the words *we* and *a*, and they shared the word *saw* with their teacher. (Most likely, however, many students will remember *saw* after the book is completed because of the repetition.)

If you look closely at the word *giraffe*, you can see that the teacher wrote *gi* and then had students share the pen for *raff*. The teacher then put in the final *e*. Knowing that the letter *g* can have a soft sound like the letter *j* was not a teaching priority for this prekindergarten classroom. Talking about letter names, practicing letter formation, and thinking about letter–sound relationships, in addition to saying words slowly, are central points in every interactive writing lesson for PreK students.

Thank-You Letter (Kindergarten)

Finally, the artwork that supports the text added meaning and beauty to the piece. The teacher included photographs of a giraffe so that students could use visuals to support their paintings. The end result was an illustrated text that was added to the classroom library (after being displayed on a bulletin board). Moreover, as students reread the text during literacy centers, the piece served as an artifact of their shared learning and holds deep meaning.

Kindergarten

The kindergarten piece shows the power of writing for real-world purposes. Teaching students when, why, and how to write a thank-you letter can start in the earliest grades. In this example, which was written over two days, kindergartners showed their appreciation for parents coming and helping in their classrooms during a Halloween celebration. Again, because the experience was shared by the entire class, everyone had ideas to offer.

The discussion of the event, which focused on *how* the parents helped, allowed the writing to expand from one sentence into two. Simple sentences were combined to include both *coming* and *helping* in the same sentence. The words *games* and *crafts* offered details of what was most appreciated.

The features of personal letter writing are spotted easily. The class began with the date and then included a greeting, a body, and a closing. Commas were used in concrete ways (within the date, greeting, and closing). Words and word parts were written by a range of students along with the teacher. Grammar goals included the use of *-ing* and *-ed*. The words were well spaced, spelled correctly, and written neatly. Concepts about print, hearing and recording sounds in words, emphasis on reading and writing high-frequency words, as well as handwriting instruction are embedded in every interactive writing lesson for these emergent writers. Finally, photographs of the special Halloween event were pasted within the letter to deepen the letter's message. The letter was hung on the classroom door so that parents could read it.

Science Research (Grade 1)

Grade 1

In this example, first-grade students completed a number of science investigations to build their knowledge around properties of matter. The interactive writing piece was a culmination of what they learned from each investigation. It is explanatory writing, yet it also represents their research findings. The piece represents nicely how interactive writing can be used in all content areas and is an excellent tool to review and reinforce the key concepts of lessons in any subject area.

This writing also highlights how the process evolves over days or even weeks. In this case, the piece was built out over seven sessions. The title and leading question were written on day one. Then, additional facts were written (one per day) as the week progressed. In each lesson, the idea was discussed first, and then the precise language was agreed upon through carefully negotiated teaching in order to best convey the information.

Throughout the discussion, the teacher reminded students to include scientific terms wherever possible. The rich discussion around the properties of solids and liquids included vocabulary such as *shape*, *pour*, *roll*, *stack*, *sink*, *float*, and *mix*. Clarity around ideas required the writing to distinguish what is true of "all" solids and liquids and what is true of "some." Comparative phrases such as "harder than others" and comparative sentences such as "Some liquids mix with water and some do not" are strong models of science writing based on research.

Once a sentence was composed, students shared the pen with the teacher to write it accurately. As in all interactive writing pieces, spelling, grammar, and punctuation are conventional. Mistakes were edited with the help of white correction tape. Many high-frequency words were included (e.g., *and*, *all*, *you*, *did*, *can*, *do*, *not*). Longer and more complex words (e.g., *water*, *harder*, *float*) offered additional spelling opportunities around letter clusters and word parts, such as the suffix *-er*. The addition of drawings and diagrams provides an exemplar for students to study and follow for future independent science writing.

Grade 2

The second-grade selection shows how writing becomes more fluent as students grow and develop. This class of English learners (ELs) worked collaboratively to retell the key events from *The True Story of the 3 Little Pigs!* (Scieszka, 1989), a book they had read together recently. Several days were needed to complete this piece. Students wrote two to four sentences during each session. The extended length of text provided more challenge to these older students. These ELs benefited from the considerable language support that is infused into interactive writing through meaningful talk.

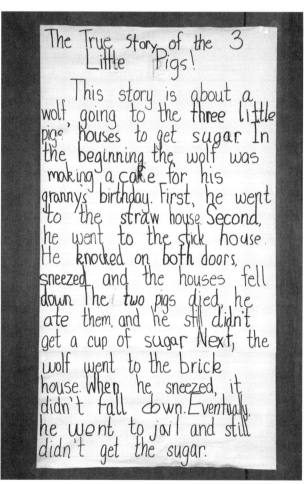

Book Summary (Grade 2)

9

Throughout the process, the teacher and her students discussed the difference between retelling every event and retelling only the most important events. In many ways, it shows beginning work around how to write a summary. Knowing which points to include, leave out, combine, or paraphrase is challenging and complex work. The teacher-led discussion around this craft required thoughtful negotiation and appropriate scaffolding. There was a great deal of teaching going on!

The result was a nine-sentence summary of the book that included a range of sentences and phrases ("In the beginning," "First," etc.) to guide readers. The organization engages and satisfies us. The ideas are helpful and relevant to our understanding. Combining the events of pig one and pig two is an efficient decision. The word *eventually* stands out and helps us know that the story has almost ended.

The conventions of writing (i.e., grammar, punctuation, and spelling) used in this piece are impressive as well. The discussion around possessives in "pigs' houses" and "granny's birthday" are clear examples of plural and singular rules. Also notice that the piece is told mainly in the past tense. Working through past-tense verbs allowed for regular and irregular endings to be practiced. Using commas to introduce clauses reminded writers to pause and use a natural flow of language. For spelling, the teacher often wrote the easy high-frequency words (e.g., "he went to the") and coached students in spelling multisyllable words and words with more complex parts to focus on spelling patterns and spelling by analogy. Consistency in letter formation and neat handwriting was emphasized.

> Panning is really popular in the gold fields because it is cheap, pans are easy to find, they are simple to use and anyone can do it. To pan, you will need the following things: a pan, gravel, dirt, a shovel, a pick-axe, a hoe and a container for your gold. First, use the hoe, pick-axe, and shovel to gather and collect the dirt. Then, take the dirt, put it in the pan and take it near the river. Dip the pan in the river and shake the pan in a swaying side-to-side motion. Next, take the pan out of the river. After that, if you have gold in your pan it should be heavier than the dirt and sink to the bottom. If there is gold in your pan, secretly put it in your pocket or container. Finally, you can take it to the bank and exchange it for lots and lots of money!

Description of Panning for Gold (Grade 3)

Grade 3

Similar to the first-grade piece, the third-grade sample shows how interactive writing works well in different content areas and can be supported by technology. It also highlights how technology supports the method. The students in this third-grade classroom were studying the Gold Rush of 1849, and the teacher used the unit's content and interactive writing to teach students about writing several different genres, including historical fiction, narrative, and descriptive writing. In this piece, he focused on descriptive writing through a detailed how-to paragraph.

Before the writing began, the teacher laid out a plan for his students. He had several expectations of what needed to be included. He captured additional notes from a quick five-minute brainstorming session with the class about important ideas related to panning. These notes and ideas informed the paragraph.

The piece was written in a single session and was shared with other students in their school. It offers a detailed description of how to pan for gold and has strong organization, as the ideas are well sequenced and logically ordered. Words such as *first, then, next,* and *finally* solidify this structure. Sentences vary in length and style, which make the piece both informative and interesting. The language "shake the pan in a swaying side-to-side motion" creates a helpful image for the audience. Using technical terms such as *gravel, pick-axe, hoe,* and *shovel,* the writing clearly teaches its audience about this unique process. Additional vocabulary words such as *container, gather, dip,* and *collect* make the description even more vivid.

By the end of the piece, readers can grasp the concept of panning. The final sentences remind us that the piece was written for other children. Notions of secrecy and exchanging the gold for "lots and lots of money!" engage the audience to wonder more about this topic.

As in all interactive writing pieces, spelling is conventional and grammar and punctuation are standard. The prepositional phrases used throughout the paragraph reflect the developmental fluency these writers possess. A range of punctuation is present, including a colon, commas, periods, and a closing exclamation point.

Technology played an important role in this piece. The efficiency of keyboarding allowed the teacher to capture student ideas, phrases, and keywords as soon as they were spoken. Complex sentences were written more quickly and mistakes were corrected at the point of error. Although it is impossible for us to see any mistakes in the example, we know that many convention errors around spelling, spacing, and punctuation likely occurred as students typed.

Grade 4

This fourth-grade sample is based on a novel required within the district's English language arts curriculum. As part of the unit, students were expected to write about a character by using evidence from the text to support their ideas. Thus, interactive writing became the instructional method for showing students how to do this. Over the course of three days, the teacher and students composed and wrote this analysis. The teacher began by outlining

> In the book *Where the Mountain Meets the Moon* by Grace Lin, Ma is an important character who changes throughout the story. In the beginning, Ma is depressed. For example, she always gives a heavy sigh when Ba tells his stories.
>
> In the middle of the story, Ma is becoming less depressed and more hopeful. An example of this is when Ba tells the story of The Paper of Happiness. Ma doesn't sigh, instead she listens to his story.
>
> By the end of the story, Ma seemed joyful, grateful, and wiser. In Chapter 44 when Ma told <u>her</u> story she began to realize that she had been ungrateful and selfish by not being thankful for what she had like their food, home, family and Ba's stories.

Character Analysis (Grade 4)

the essential points to include in the opening (title, author, and character to be analyzed). Over the next two days, she worked with her students to consider the traits, thoughts, and actions of the selected character, and she guided students in how they select textual evidence to support their ideas.

First, notice the craft elements of ideas, organization, and sentence fluency. The opening sentence provides a clear and concise introduction. We know what this piece is about: a character named Ma. In the second sentence, the writing states an opinion that Ma is depressed and supports this with evidence from the text. The second paragraph builds from the first, the idea that Ma is becoming less depressed and more hopeful because she listens to Ba's stories rather than sighing. The last sentence in this paragraph has a wonderful sense of rhythm— "instead she listens to his story." These sentences flow well together, given the organization of the ideas and how well they are linked.

The final paragraph makes it clear that Ma changed in the story, as her depression gives way to feelings of joy and gratitude. Again, the piece includes solid evidence from the text that shows what Ma now appreciates in her life. The ideas are both well organized and easy to follow in these paragraphs because of the signal phrases "in the middle of the story" and "by the end of the story." These phrases serve as helpful guideposts for readers.

What's striking about this writing sample are the words selected to describe Ma. Rather than *sad*, the students opted for the word *depressed*. Describing Ma's sigh as *heavy* shows readers the depth of her sadness. As Ma begins to change, the students selected the words *more hopeful*, which pair nicely with *less depressed*. These phrases tell us that Ma is in the midst of changing, though she is not completely there yet. In the last paragraph, the words *wiser* and *realize* strengthen this analysis by suggesting that Ma has indeed undergone an experience that changed her. She has moved from being *selfish* to being *grateful*. The contrast of words paints a picture of Ma's transformation.

In terms of conventions, this piece is made up of complex sentences which are a nice stretch for these fourth-grade writers. It is also filled with commas that set off clauses and break apart the long, complex sentences. As students worked through this, the teacher often prompted them to reread their sentence and to notice where there were natural pauses in their speech. She reminded students to do this when they wrote on their own. Spelling strategies came up in natural ways, as students were not fully certain how to spell words such as *sighs*, *depressed*, and *grateful*. Further, the students focused on spelling more common words when they were unsure of whether to write *there* or *their* and discussed how to turn *story* into *stories*. These became important teaching opportunities.

Grade 5

The fifth-grade sample shows again how interactive writing can be integrated into content area teaching. This piece, created during a science period, provided students with the opportunity to practice the elements of summary writing by applying what they experienced and learned in their study of the water cycle.

> ### The Water Cycle
>
> Evaporation is when the sun's heat energy transforms liquid water into water vapor. Evaporation occurs in all bodies of water like lakes, rivers, oceans, and ponds. Next, water vapor rises into the sky and it cools, changing back into liquid form. The water vapor condenses to form clouds. Gravity pulls rain, snow, sleet, and hail back to Earth's surface in a process called precipitation. The sun is always shining; therefore, the Water Cycle is continuously moving and purifying our water.

A Summary of the Water Cycle (Grade 5)

Notice the organization of this piece. The writing unfolds in an easy-to-follow way as the steps of the water cycle are explained. As the students composed the text, they were taught and reminded to include only the main ideas rather than every detail. As ideas were suggested, the class worked together to determine whether the idea was essential. Next, notice the precise scientific terms such as *evaporation*, *water vapor*, and *precipitation*. Including this vocabulary was a teaching priority. These terms had been taught during the unit, so it was a perfect opportunity for students to apply them as they wrote this piece. Further, the teacher worked with the class to use strong verbs such as *transforms* and *rises* in order for readers to have a clearer picture of how water moves and changes through this cycle.

There are a variety of sentences in this paragraph that keeps its flow interesting. Many of the sentences include phrases and clauses that provide important details and add rhythm. For example, in the sentence "Gravity pulls rain, snow, sleet, and hail…" the final phrase is "in a process called precipitation." This final phrase brings the meaning together in a thoughtful and smooth manner.

As students worked to write this paragraph on chart paper, a range of conventions were addressed, including capitalization, spelling, and use of commas. There were many complex words to spell, such as *condenses*, *purifying*, and *continuously*. The teacher

WHAT TEACHERS ARE SAYING

Interactive writing is a part of my teaching where everyone gets excited. It's a powerful boost for my students.   —Atara (Grade 5)

used a vocabulary word bank and had students practice problem-solving strategies such as listening for familiar word parts or linking the unknown word to words they knew in order to accomplish correct spelling.

As you can also see, commas are used to call out a list of terms and to set off a single word, as in "Next, water vapor...." The final sentence includes a semicolon that separates two independent clauses while at the same time connecting them using the word *therefore* along with a comma. This sophisticated use of punctuation represents what older writers are ready to practice.

Final Thoughts

This chapter provides a beginning look at how interactive writing can have a positive influence on students' writing lives. Although the finished products are valuable and perhaps even enchanting, the interactive writing *process* is most important to understand and remember. The teaching that occurred at each step in these lessons is meaningful and intentional. The teachers knew their writers and knew what they needed to move forward. The chapters that follow provide more detail around how interactive writing fits into a comprehensive literacy model and describe how an interactive writing lesson flows. We invite you to read on to learn more about this powerful teaching method and to try it out in your classroom tomorrow.

CHAPTER 2

Understanding Interactive Writing

What are the components of interactive writing? How does it fit into your literacy teaching? Interactive writing is a singular method of instruction that holds a special place and purpose within your literacy program. This chapter identifies the basic sequence of a lesson. Discover where and how this method fits into your classroom's writing program.

Interactive writing may be used for a range of authentic purposes such as writing a letter, recording a science investigation, summarizing or responding to a read-aloud, or writing about a mathematical problem. Because students participate actively in the writing of the text and read it many times in the process, they create text that is accessible and readable. The text is written neatly and accurately and uses conventional spelling, grammar, capitalization, and punctuation. Many of the pieces created become valuable teaching resources for future reading and writing instruction. However, although the writing *products* created during interactive writing are important, it is the *process* that is most valuable for advancing students' independent writing.

An Interactive Writing Lesson: The Basic Sequence

Interactive writing is organized and structured; it follows a predictable sequence with each step holding important value. Table 1 gives an overview of the method and names and describes each step within it. That said, there is room for flexibility, and adaptations between the grade levels are expected. As you learn and practice this method, you will find that you adjust it to fit your teaching style an your students' writing needs.

WHAT TEACHERS ARE SAYING

Because lessons are engaging, relevant, and provide scaffolded instruction, interactive writing is an ideal approach for providing all students with the literacy skills necessary for independent writing and reading ... [A] great sense of accomplishment and pride is instilled in them.

—Jeff (PreK)

Table 1 An Overview of an Interactive Writing Lesson

Interactive writing: a dynamic instructional method during which the teacher serves as the expert writer for students as they work together to construct a meaningful text while simultaneously discussing the details of the writing process. Together, they plan, compose, and review text in a variety of genres. The "interactive" piece involves group collaboration in planning and composing the writing through guided conversation and a unique "sharing the pen" technique where students do the actual scribing.	

Experience	• The writing is motivated and informed by a shared classroom experience
	• A range of everyday classroom experiences can be harnessed for interactive writing, such as the following:
	  o A read-aloud
	  o Curriculum content (e.g., topics studied in English language arts, math, science, or history)
	  o Special events (e.g., assembly, field trip, classroom celebration)
	  o Classroom routines or processes

Prewrite	• Teacher and students plan the writing piece by considering the following:
	  o Purpose
	  o Intended audience for the piece
	  o Best structure for the piece
	• Prewrite becomes more formal and detailed as writers develop

Compose	• Teacher skillfully facilitates a discussion focused on the craft of writing by strategically engaging and guiding students to compose a single sentence
	• Together, teacher and the students do the following:
	  o Focus on important craft elements (organization, word choice, sentence fluency, vocabulary, and voice)
	  o Negotiate the precise language of the text

Share the Pen	• Teacher and the students write the message on paper (or on the screen) through an innovative approach called Share the Pen (or Share the Keyboard) • Teacher writes/types parts of the message and then selects students to write/type at points of high instructional value • Editing of conventions is done by the student (with teacher support) at the point of error so that the final piece is in "publishable" form

Review	• The class briefly revisits the written piece to reinforce particular concepts learned about the craft and conventions of writing
	  o *Part 1:* Students interact with the piece to review a few of the key principles taught
	  o *Part 2:* Teacher summarizes the key craft and convention principles that were practiced during the lesson
	• Teacher reminds students how to apply the lesson principles to their own writing

Extend	• The completed writing piece becomes an instructional tool that supports and advances students' literacy development
	• It can be extended in multiple ways, such as the following:
	  o Rereading it for multiple purposes (e.g., focus on concepts about print, focus on high-frequency words, focus on unique vocabulary)
	  o Highlighting the features of the genre practiced
	  o Connecting the piece to students' independent writing
	  o Incorporating visuals
	  o Sharing the piece with its intended audience

Experience: Interactive writing is motivated and informed by a shared classroom experience. Many experiences meet this requirement, such as a book read together, the content studied in a science or social studies lesson, or a class field trip or school assembly. By writing about a shared experience, every student in the class has a voice and can contribute to the final writing piece.

Prewrite: Before writing, an author must first consider the function and form of the writing. Together you and the students think about who your audience is, the overall message you want to convey, and why it is important. For example, after a field trip you might decide to write a letter to thank the hosts, a retelling to share your experience, or a report to share what you learned.

Compose: As you compose the piece, you and your students focus on the craft of writing while discussing the specific content. Students share their ideas while you help them negotiate the precise language of the text. Specifically, you synthesize their ideas, help them organize their thoughts as writers, propose vocabulary or language that advances the ideas, and, in some cases, suggest the "final sentence" based on your discussion. You might also use think-alouds to model for students why that sentence is most appropriate.

Share the Pen: This step focuses on the conventions of writing. The text is written with an innovative technique unique to interactive writing in which you and the students take turns with the pen or marker. With older and more fluent writers, Share the Pen can be modified to become Share the Keyboard, as you and your students type using a keyboard or touch screen with text displayed on a screen or interactive whiteboard. In all cases, you write or type some text and then choose students to write or type at points of high instructional value.

Share the Pen (Grade 3)

17

Share the Keyboard (Grade 5)

Editing of conventions is done at the point of error or at the end of each sentence. Similar to the Compose phase, you may use think-alouds to model specific points about conventions that are emerging in the lesson, such as letter formation, spelling, spacing, or punctuation.

Review: After the piece is written completely, you revisit it briefly with your students to highlight a few important instructional points. First, you guide your students to interact with the message again by looking for examples of the key principles taught explicitly during the lesson. Then, you conclude by summarizing what was learned about the craft and conventions of writing. The final teaching move during Review is to connect the lesson to your students' own writing. This connection helps students consolidate their new learning and understand why it matters. Your students have co-constructed the writing piece and understand it fully. Because of this, you can reinforce the key writing principles that they will now be expected to use when writing their own pieces.

Extend: During Extend the completed writing piece is used as an instructional tool to support and advance students' literacy development. For example, you might reread the piece in order to highlight important concepts about print, to point out unique vocabulary, or to support fluent oral reading. Or your students might illustrate final pieces with collages, photographs, or other forms of art that match the style of writing. You might decide to mount the writing and make it into a class book or mural that the students can reread regularly. The final piece can often become an exemplar of a particular genre you are studying. Sharing the writing with the intended audience (e.g., the school community or with families in a newsletter) is another way of extending the text. And, your students might also write similar pieces on their own.

WHAT TEACHERS ARE SAYING

The walls of my room are covered in all of this writing we do chronicling the many things we experience and study during the year, so both the process and products help create a real community in my class around literacy.

—Katie (Grade 1)

Lesson Frequency and Duration

For students of any age, interactive writing lessons need to be fast paced and demand a high level of engagement. It is recommended as a daily practice in grades PreK–1 (Roth & Guinee, 2011). Young students have much to learn about how print works, so frequent lessons are essential. At the beginning of second grade, it likely may be that students still need and will benefit from daily interactive writing lessons. However, as the second-grade year progresses, the practice might shift and be needed each week or several times each week rather than every day. For more advanced writers, interactive writing lessons are scheduled as needed.

At the beginning of the year when teachers in grades 3–5 launch their literacy block, they might start by using interactive writing three times per week in order to introduce and establish the sequence and to support the writing process. Then, as the writing curriculum moves forward, the method can be used periodically to highlight key writing principles or to teach specific features of different genres.

For example, when working through a unit of study on nonfiction writing, interactive writing can be a helpful method for guiding students in how to use language precisely or convey facts succinctly. This teaching might require two or three days in a row of interactive writing. Then, once the piece is written, students can use it as an exemplar. At that point, it may work well for you to shift and use other instructional approaches to teach them about nonfiction writing (e.g., focus lessons, modeled writing, independent practice). And it may be that you pivot back to interactive writing as the unit evolves.

To simplify this difference in frequency, think about how a teacher initially prepares what to teach during interactive writing: Prekindergarten through first-grade teachers often begin planning by asking themselves, "What will we write about in interactive writing today?" Around the middle of second grade to the beginning of third grade, the question becomes, "What do I need to teach my students about writing today, this week, or within this unit of study, and how will the method of interactive writing help support this writing principle?"

Furthermore, although the lessons might occur less frequently in an upper elementary classroom, each lesson may be longer in duration than in a classroom of emergent writers. Whereas a lesson might average 10 to 15 minutes a day in grade 1 (Roth & Guinee 2011), in grades 2–5, lessons generally last between 20 and 30 minutes. Because students' attention spans are greater, they are able to absorb more in one lesson. They are also able to generate more text in one lesson because they are more fluent writers. The lessons become progressively more in-depth as the writers advance, and thus interactive writing lessons require more time.

Interactive Writing: A Valuable Component in a Comprehensive Literacy Framework

Interactive writing is most effective when integrated into a comprehensive literacy framework that supports writers in a variety of important ways. In this section, we make connections between interactive writing and (a) the writing process, (b) the gradual release of responsibility model, and (c) language and reading development.

Interactive Writing and the Writing Process

Writing is a recursive process of generating and planning ideas, drafting, revising and editing, and publishing. Students need to be taught these processes explicitly and be given time to practice them. The processes become more sophisticated and complex as writers develop. Although there is a general sequence of how a piece of writing progresses, the writing process is not lockstep. Rather, it is fluid and unique for each writer and each piece of writing (Graham & Harris, 2013). Real writers employ these processes at the precise moment when they are needed. For example, when we draft new ideas, frequently we are revising at the same time. Moreover, the prominent use of word processing technology allows drafting, revising, and editing to be more integrated than ever before.

Interactive writing connects well with the writing process. Although the lesson sequence as a whole does not mirror it, the recursive phases of the writing process are found within the lesson steps. For example, you and your students are generating and planning as you brainstorm together during Prewrite. During Compose, there will be moments to plan, draft, and revise your thinking as you discuss word choice, sentence structure, voice, and organization of the piece. Then, as you share the pen with students, opportunities to edit arise as you make in-the-moment decisions about spelling, spacing, and punctuation. Any errors are corrected in real time.

In addition, the think-alouds you do within an interactive writing lesson can highlight the writing process. This lets students see and hear how real writers turn thoughts and conversation into written text. The final piece created during interactive writing is already in "publishable" form. When you extend the piece by displaying it in an attractive way or by sharing it with a larger audience, you further reinforce the publishing phase of the writing process.

Balanced Writing Instruction Within a Gradual Release of Responsibility Model

Students need multiple opportunities to learn how to write (Graham & Harris, 2013). They develop as writers when they routinely do the following:

- Write for a wide range of purposes and audiences
- Learn about the craft and conventions of writing
- Practice the writing processes of plan, draft, revise, edit, and publish
- Read and analyze models of well-crafted stories or informational writing
- "Listen in" on the expert thinking of a writer in various stages of crafting a piece
- Learn and practice the rules and nuances of the English language
- Receive and act on specific feedback about their writing

The gradual release of responsibility model is a helpful instructional approach for addressing these writing expectations (see Figure 1). This model advances the idea that students move toward independence with intentional scaffolding from the teacher. Our students gradually take on more of the cognitive "responsibility" as we support them in modeled, shared, and guided

Figure 1 Interactive Writing Within the Gradual Release of Responsibility Model

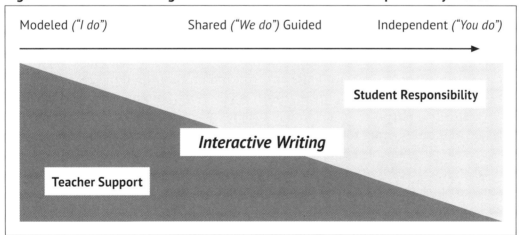

Note. Adapted from "The Instruction of Reading Comprehension," by P.D. Pearson and M.C. Gallagher, 1983, *Contemporary Educational Psychology, 8*(3), 317–344.

experiences. Ultimately, we release full responsibility to them when they move into independent experiences (Pearson & Gallagher, 1983; Vygotsky, 1978).

Said more simply, the gradual release model starts with an "I do" (teacher modeling, shifts to a "we do" (teacher and students together in shared and guided experiences), and culminates with a "you do" (student independent practice). Explicit instruction is present throughout this framework. When the task becomes more complex, we take back responsibility by offering more support and guidance. But the ultimate goal is to release responsibility to our students (when they are ready) in an effort to increase their independent capabilities.

When we think about our writing instruction, the gradual release model is our compass. We are always mindful of the ultimate goal: to teach students the skills and strategies they need to write well on their own in school and for life. At times, our teaching practices provide significant support and guidance for them. These practices include modeling our own writing, providing explicit instruction around writing craft and conventions through focus or minilessons, or analyzing exemplar pieces written by published authors.

At other times our instruction must shift as we release parts of the writing "work" to students. For example, in shared writing, we work with students to plan and compose a text together through a skillfully facilitated discussion. Then, we do the actual writing for them. Another common writing practice, morning message, may include both "I do" and "we do" opportunities; however, in most instances, you have planned or written out the text ahead of the lesson. On the other end of the continuum, we often have students write independently. During these times, we offer minimal support and allow students to practice the writing process as they draft, revise, and edit their own writing in many genres.

In many classrooms, teachers use writers' workshop to advance both the natural flow of the writing process and the gradual release of responsibility. Within writers' workshop, students are working on their own pieces as they practice what real writers do: plan, draft, revise, edit, and publish. The pieces have real-world purposes (e.g., students' own collection, a class book, a hallway display) and are written for a wide range of audiences (e.g., the teacher, other classmates, parents, local community organization) (Graham et al., 2013).

During writers' workshop, students move back and forth within the gradual release framework. For example, during a writing conference, you may heavily scaffold instruction as you model for the student a new revision skill. Or a student may have full independence as she edits her writing using a checklist created earlier during whole-class instruction.

Interactive writing is a writing practice that falls within the "we do" portion of the gradual release of responsibility model. It is a unique practice in that it offers a high level of teacher support while involving students throughout the entire writing process. The technique of literally "sharing the pen" is special to this method. Although it yields big results in students' independent writing, interactive writing is not meant to be the sole form of writing instruction. Ideally, it works best when nested between and among other modeled, shared, and independent writing experiences.

As teachers, we consider and select our instructional practices thoughtfully and recognize how they will support and advance our student writers. We also notice how much teacher support each practice requires. If we find ourselves frequently modeling for students with limited time for shared or guided experiences, students may not fully grasp or own the concepts we are teaching. Or, if we expect independence before students have had ample time to practice a skill with teacher support, we may not see students' independent writing improving.

We believe in using interactive writing regularly because it is an effective practice that provides the essential step between high support and independence. It complements and enhances any other writing practices you use. Overall, the gradual release of responsibility model keeps us grounded in our work to support independent writing. It reminds us that our instruction must be both systematic and balanced.

Connecting Interactive Writing With Language and Reading Development

Interactive writing is a multifaceted approach to instruction that brings together all aspects of a literacy framework in every lesson (McCarrier et al., 2000). In addition to the independent writing benefits, interactive writing offers instructional opportunities in oral language, word study, and reading development simultaneously. Oral language is practiced and refined throughout interactive writing as you and the students engage in rich and rigorous conversations. Throughout your discussions, vocabulary is introduced, grammar is considered, and oral fluency is practiced.

Discussion During Compose (Grade 5)

Discussion During Share the Pen (Kindergarten)

For students learning English, the oral language benefits are uniquely powerful. In a "safe practice" environment, these students can listen to and engage in a meaningful discussion that culminates in a written text. Observing how talk translates into written text is powerful for these emergent writers (Gibbons, 2015). Moreover, the written piece holds meaning for them because the writing experience is interactive and they have ownership of the final product.

Reading and writing are reciprocal processes. As we teach students to read, we encourage them to take words apart. As we teach students to write, we guide them to put sounds and letters together. Experiencing these "breaking down" and "building up" processes within a single lesson reinforces their literacy learning (Clay, 1991).

Throughout an interactive writing lesson, students are practicing these give-and-take processes. They are reading as they craft and refine their writing. There is emphasis on letter or letter-cluster sounds and high-frequency words, both items of knowledge that will help improve students' reading and writing at the same time. There will also be moments for you to pull from your word study or spelling programs as you and the students consider the best words and phrases to include.

Further, the final written piece becomes an exemplar to be read repeatedly and comprehended by all. As they reread the co-constructed piece both during and after the lesson, students have a chance

Student Guides Peers to Reread During Review (Grade 3)

to practice fluency *and* to read a range of texts in different genres. Students at every level are learning all this as they simultaneously work through the writing process.

A skillfully taught interactive writing lesson pulls from your entire literacy curriculum. Because you know where your students are in their reading and word study development, you can anticipate where and when to make these connections. Student learning is maximized as a result of this authentic and integrated approach.

Final Thoughts

Now that you have an initial vision of the product and the process of interactive writing and an understanding of where and how it fits in with your literacy teaching, you are ready to dive in and learn how to implement this practice effectively in your classroom. In Section Two (Chapters 3–8), you will work through each step of an interactive writing lesson in depth and learn how to implement this approach to meet your students' unique grade-level needs. Taken together, these chapters will coach you as you first master the technique at the procedural level. Then, once the basic routines and lesson format are in place, you can develop your expertise and refine your craft by fine-tuning the way teaching decisions are made before and throughout the lesson.

But first, take a few minutes to reflect on your current approach to writing instruction. Use the questions and the chart in Figure 2 to organize your thinking:

- What teaching practices do I use regularly to help my students become better writers?
- Why do I use these practices? How do they support my student writers?
- How do I balance the "I do," "we do," and "you do" teaching practices over the course of a day? A week? A unit of study?

Figure 2 Balanced Writing Instruction Within the Gradual Release of Responsibility

Writing Practice	How Often Do I Use This?	Teacher Support (High-Medium-Low)	Student Responsibility (High-Medium-Low)

Working Through Each Part of an Interactive Writing Lesson

CHAPTER 3

Experience

What do we write about during interactive writing? Writers write about what they know and experience! This chapter looks closely at how and why to anchor interactive writing in a shared classroom experience.

Choosing a topic to write about often can be the biggest challenge writers face. As adults, we can envision that blank page in front of us and feel the overwhelming sense of "being stuck." In our teaching, perhaps we have heard students say, "I don't know what to write." Or, even more troubling, "I have nothing interesting to write about." Realizing that ideas for writing can come from our ordinary, everyday happenings is an empowering step for developing writers. Interactive writing embraces this.

In this chapter, we describe the many types of experiences that work well for interactive writing. These experiences, shared by *all* students, can inform a variety of writing pieces. They also set the stage for student ownership of the piece.

Experience: Where It All Begins

Ideas for an interactive writing piece come from everyday classroom and student experiences. This models what we know is a best practice: Writers write about what they know (Bromley, 2011). They write about their own lives, the people they meet and know, the world around them, or ideas they have researched or studied. This is the theory behind Experience. Experience matters because it sets the stage for an authentic, whole-class writing lesson. Experience matters because it models for students what "real" writers do—they write about what they know and *experience*.

Expert Voices: The Power of *Shared* Experience

Interactive writing is, at its heart, a collaborative activity that models a powerful concept: You and your students are a community of writers (Nolen, 2007). Thus, the piece to be written is motivated and informed by a *shared* classroom experience. Because all students have participated in the experience, they all have "something to say" about it. The topic holds relevance and meaning for the entire class. This inclusive process sets the stage for a rich and rigorous composing session where *every* child can participate with authority and expertise.

A shared experience is especially helpful for ELs who may be developing language and literacy skills in multiple languages. The experience is reinforced in a timely manner through talk and then extends into writing. These well-sequenced events (i.e., shared experience, talk, and writing) lead to deeper comprehension, expanded language, and strengthened writing skills (Gibbons, 2015).

Endless Opportunities for Writing: Harnessing the Everyday Experience

There are endless experiences that work well for interactive writing. When teachers realize this, they often consider this versatility one of the strengths of the interactive writing method. It is not about creating a "big project" or planning a grand event that then evolves into interactive writing. Rather, it is about selecting, capturing, and recording the meaningful events that students experience each day at school. You use the interactive writing method to maximize these ordinary yet worthwhile moments by keeping your eyes and ears tuned to the potential they hold for teaching students about writing.

As you browse the images of interactive writing in this chapter and throughout the book, you will discover a range of experiences that provide a multitude of ideas. They include field trips, science investigations, author studies, science and social studies topics of study, math projects, books read aloud in class, class assemblies, classroom routines and procedures, and special school events.

Table 2 lists possible experiences that can fuel a productive interactive writing lesson. We organize these experiences into particular subject areas, special events, and everyday routines. Students at any age are capable of writing about a shared experience. What changes over time is the complexity of the writing.

English Language Arts

Interactive writing provides students the opportunity to "explore and extend the meaning of literature" (McCarrier et al., 2000, p. 123). Your reading block offers a range of authentic shared experiences that can launch an engaging

Table 2 Possible Experiences for Interactive Writing

Subject/Area	Possible Experiences
English Language Arts	• Author studies • Genre studies • Texts shared during whole-class read-alouds
Math, Social Studies, and Science	• Any grade-level content • Books or texts shared in whole-class read-alouds • Analysis of a primary or secondary source document • An investigation
Special Events	• Assembly • Field trip • Guest speaker • Class celebration • Unique activities and projects (e.g., cooking, art)
Routines and Processes	• Classroom rules, routines, and procedures • Problem-solving strategies

interactive writing lesson. A book read and discussed aloud is a natural place to start. As a class, you and your students can (and should!) write about reading in a variety of ways with the goal of helping students to "expand their thinking and improve their ability to reflect on a text" (Pinnell & Fountas, 2011, p. 70). Both fiction and nonfiction texts, whether through read-alouds or shared readings, can be the core of valuable interactive writing experiences. There are many ways to respond to a book, including retellings, summaries, or an informational piece. Similarly, as you read and analyze multiple texts by the same author, students come to know and appreciate an author's style. Interactive writing is a perfect opportunity to write about how an author presents his or her ideas or uses illustrations.

Another opportunity during English language arts is genre study. When you and your students read and study a particular genre of text (e.g., biographies, science fiction), you often discover the important characteristics about that genre. These features are important for students

Interactive Read-Aloud (Grade 1)

There are several events that led to the invention of The Slinky. First, Richard James was hired by the U.S. Navy to invent a device that stabalizes ships. When he failed he used springs to help with the resistance. Then, he accidentally knocked the spring off the shelf. Instead of it falling flat to the ground like he thought, it walked coil over coil off the shelf. Richard tried that over and over again to make sure that it repeated the same moves, and it worked.

Later, Richard went home to show his wife Betty what he discovered. They tested it in different spots around the house to see if it would work anywhere. It walked coil over coil in many locations. Betty and Richard realized that the spring could be a toy. Betty looked in the dictionary and came up with a name for it, "The Slinky".

Shared Reading of Informational Text (Grade 4)

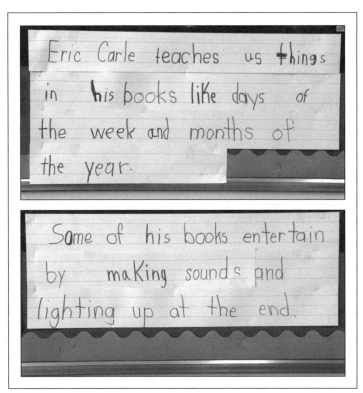

Eric Carle teaches us things in his books like days of the week and months of the year.

Some of his books entertain by making sounds and lighting up at the end.

Author Study (Grade 1)

to know and remember as they expand their reading repertoire. Interactive writing can be used to capture these discoveries. For example, if your class is reading a mystery together, it is likely that students notice how and when the author includes important details or clues. As readers become aware of how a genre "works," interactive writing can be the method used to solidify these shared understandings.

Math, Social Studies, and Science

The topics in math, social studies, and science lend themselves well to interactive writing. The content is rich with possibilities for a writing lesson! In math, you might use the learning that was done in a lesson as the basis for a narrative piece. You might also work as a class to define an important mathematical concept that students are studying.

In social studies, you can use your curriculum to inform a range of interactive writing pieces. The study of historical and current events, world cultures, geography, or influential leaders represents a whole-class, content-rich experience. This experience can flow nicely into an interactive writing lesson focused on informational writing. Science content across grades PreK through 5 can also inform interactive writing sessions. You can see in the writing samples how students at all ages are able to write about science concepts in increasingly more sophisticated ways as their knowledge grows. We see this writing progression clearly as their pieces become longer, their sentences become more complex, and their vocabulary expands.

Further, science labs or investigations offer another distinct experience. In all cases, the writing you do across content areas will be filled with precise vocabulary and terminology. You will find that integrating interactive writing with content area teaching is both efficient and beneficial. As you move through your curriculum, the method becomes a natural moment where students practice a specific type of writing *and* deepen their understanding of the concepts they are learning. Truly, this is a win–win experience!

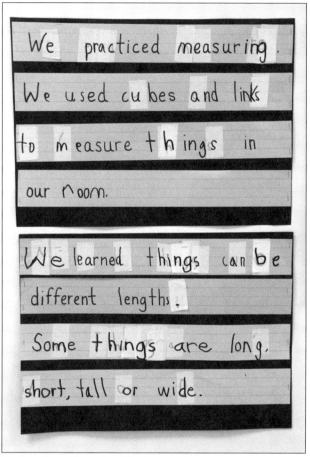

Math Unit on Measuring (Kindergarten)

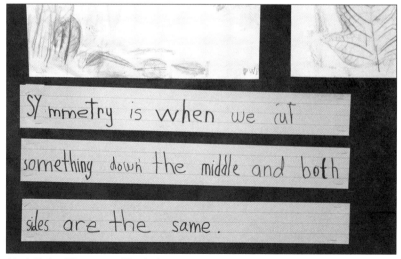

Math Unit of Symmetry (Grade 1)

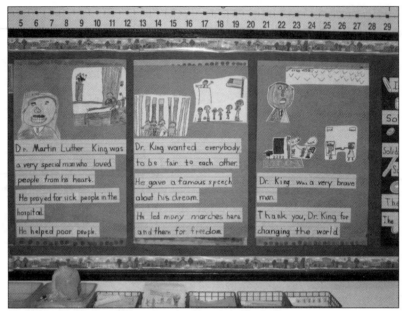

Social Studies Unit on African American Leaders (Grade 1)

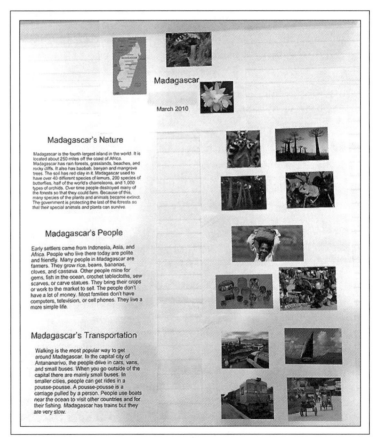

Social Studies Unit on World Cultures (Grade 3)

Science Unit on the Five Senses (PreK)

Science Unit on Plants (Grade 1)

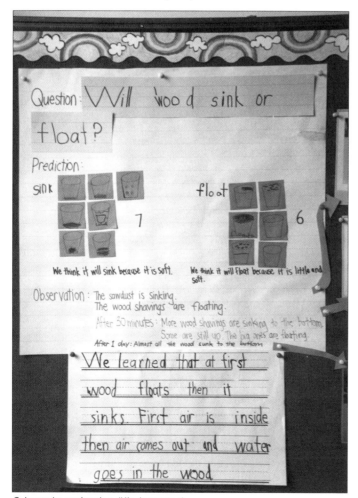

Science Investigation (Kindergarten)

Read-Aloud of Informational Texts (Grade 3)

Rocking the Rock Cycle

The three types of rocks that make up Earth's crust are sedimentary, igneous, and metamorphic rocks. The Rock Cycle forms these rocks which come in diverse shapes, colors, and sizes. Sedimentary rocks are formed when sediments such as weathered rocks, sand, and dead organisms experience forceful pressure and are cemented into layers. Sedimentary rocks transform into metamorphic rock when the rock encounters extreme heat and pressure. Igneous rocks are created when magma, or molten rock, cools and solidifies. A process that morphs igneous rocks into sediment is called weathering and erosion. Igneous rocks can mutate into metamorphic rocks when they undergo a great amount of heat and pressure. Metamorphic rocks are created from igneous and sedimentary rocks that have been exposed to an extravagant amount of heat and pressure. The melting process alters metamorphic rocks by changing them into magma, while weathering and erosion deconstruct metamorphic rocks into sediment. The Rock Cycle includes numerous processes that form and modify Earth's crust.

Science Unit on the Rock Cycle (Grade 5)

Special Events

Every classroom encounters special events as the year unfolds. Often we record these activities through photos or videos. Interactive writing connects beautifully with these moments. What better way to remember and celebrate a special occasion than by writing about it? Schoolwide assemblies are quite common and are events that students treasure for many years. Whether students perform in one or attend one, there is plenty to remember, and students are often enthusiastic in their recollections.

Field trips hold similar value, as students move outside of their classroom walls and experience their larger world. Writing about journeys (big or small) allows students to include vivid detail. Classroom celebrations of holidays, guest speakers, and unique activities also offer noteworthy opportunities for interactive writing.

Routines and Processes

The daily routines and processes you want your students to know and demonstrate will become more systematic when they are written down and displayed. Rather than write these *for* your students, use interactive writing to write them *with* your students. For example, you might work with your students to co-construct the rules for their classroom. Even our youngest students have something to say about how a well-managed classroom should look, sound, and feel. Additionally, when you or your students experience any type of classroom challenge or problem over the course of the school year, interactive writing can be a powerful tool for recording a strategy or solution. These dilemmas can range from academic to behavioral. Regardless of the specific issue, interactive writing can be an instructive approach to solving a problem as you and your students co-construct the strategies for resolving it.

On Thursday, May 9th, 2013, our class precisely performed our spring concert. This concert was presented by 2nd and 3rd graders and was held in the auditorium. Before it started, we were feeling a little scared and nervous, but that didn't bother us because we knew it was going to be fantastic.

Now, do you want to know about how our awesome and amazing spring concert began? First, our parents brought us to school and dropped us off in the classroom. Next, we walked in a straight and quiet line to the auditorium. When we got there, we waited in the wings until it was our turn to perform Hot Cross Buns on the recorder. Then, Mr. Dennison told us to go up to the risers and we listened to the other classes perform. After that, we sung Cherry Blossom, which was a sad song. We couldn't wait to perform The Whack Attack. It is a very fun and energetic song. Then we sang a song called Bring Me Sunshine using sign language, and we were joined by the second graders. Later on we gave flowers to our music teachers and returned to our classroom. Although we were exhausted and hungry, we were very proud of our performance and happy to go home. We are definitely excited about performing again next year.

Student-Performed Assembly (Grade 3)

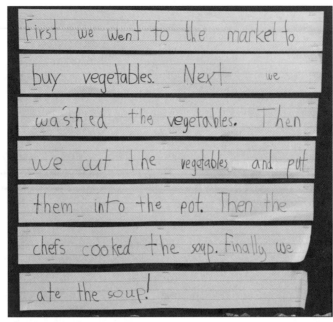

First we went to the market to buy vegetables. Next we washed the vegetables. Then we cut the vegetables and put them into the pot. Then the chefs cooked the soup. Finally we ate the soup!

Field Trip and Cooking Activity (Kindergarten)

I. Homes

Houses are made out of bricks and wood in our neighborhood People live in apartments and houses with three floors. Many houses have backyards

Walking Tour of Neighborhood (Grade 1)

Every fourth grader should have a chance to go to the art museum. One reason is that learning outside of the classroom is interesting and exciting. We learned how art can tell a story. For example, we saw a painting of a girl who falls in love with a crusader, her father's enemy. If you allow your students to go to an art museum, they will also learn about the feelings and emotions of an artist and how they express these in their artwork. An example of this is when Pablo Picasso was in his "blue" period, he painted pictures using dark tones to express his depressed feelings and mood. These are the reasons why every fourth grader should have an opportunity to visit an art museum.

Field Trip to Art Museum (Grade 4)

Celebration of Halloween (PreK)

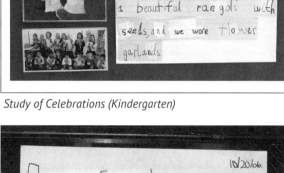

Study of Celebrations (Kindergarten)

It's Christmas!

Christmas is a happy time that comes only once a year when families come together and celebrate their traditions. On Christmas morning, many families gather around the beautifully decorated tree seeing what they got from Santa Claus. Santa Claus is a Christmas mascot, who flies in a sleigh, using reindeer to deliver gifts such as gift cards, money, games, clothes and much more to the well-behaved children of the world. On Christmas night, many families gather around the table for a wonderful family dinner. Christmas is about spending joyful moments and sharing laughter with your family and friends.

Study of Winter Holidays (Grade 4)

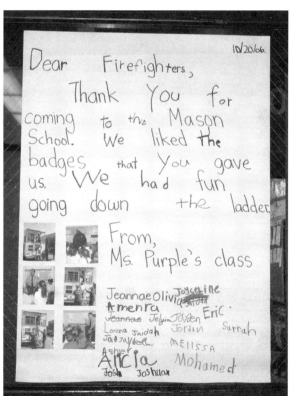

Visit From Local Firefighters (Grade 1)

How to Make a Stir-fry

Ingrediants:
- noodles
- 3-5 different vegetables
- soy sauce
- oil
- ginger and/or garlic

Materials Needed:
- stove top or burner
- knife
- pan
- wooden spoon and/or spatula
- cutting board

1. Wash the vegetables.
2. Cut the vegetables.
3. If you are using ginger, peel it.
4. If you are using garlic, peel and chop it.
5. Put the pan on the burner.
6. Turn the burner on.
7. Put a tablespoon of oil in the pan.
8. Add the vegetables and other food.
9. Stir and cook for 10 minutes.

Cooking Activity as Part of a Social Studies Unit on China (Grade 2)

Room 8 Rules

We treat others the way we want to be treated.

We use quiet voices while we are working.

We keep our hands and our bodies to ourselves.

We listen to the teachers.

We take care of our classroom.

We make good choices everyday.

Generating Classroom Rules (Grade 1)

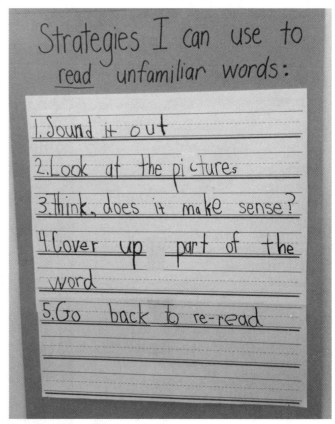

Strategies I can use to read unfamiliar words:

1. Sound it out
2. Look at the pictures
3. Think, does it make sense?
4. Cover up part of the word
5. Go back to re-read

Learning to Read (Kindergarten)

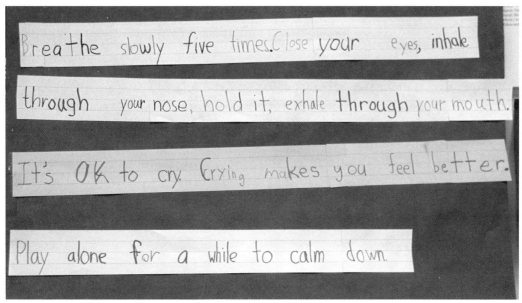

Learning Strategies for Calming Down (Grade 1)

Choosing Experiences for Interactive Writing

When deciding what experiences to use for interactive writing, consider the following guidelines. First, select an experience that is meaningful for you and your students. By this we mean it must be worth writing about! This importance may be based in the content area knowledge you want your students to know and remember or it may support the strategies, routines, or processes that you want them to follow. Or it may be based in special events or moments that bond your classroom community in important ways. Whatever the rationale, the motivation and engagement to write occur when the topic holds value for students. As you plan, you might ask yourself questions such as the following:

- What are we studying right now in science? Social studies? Math? English language arts? Do any of the important concepts foster writing connections?

- What events beyond the classroom are happening this week or month? A special assembly? A visitor to the school or classroom? Is there something we want to record to remember? A person deserving a thank-you note?

WHAT TEACHERS ARE SAYING

I'm always looking at the week ahead and thinking about what we can write about next. Almost everything we do can be turned into an experience for interactive writing.

—Jennifer (Literacy Coach)

- Are there classroom management routines or procedures that need to be written down? What reminders should we record for the classroom to run smoothly?

Next, think about the writing goals you have for your students. Often these expectations are anchored in your school's or district's curriculum. As you select an experience, be sure to think ahead about how it supports and aligns with your overall writing curriculum. Finally, identify the specific writing strategies or techniques you want your students to learn and practice. The experience you select to write about should offer the precise instructional opportunities they need.

Final Thoughts

Selecting a shared experience is the first step in an interactive writing lesson. Experience will propel the lesson forward, as students speak with confidence and authority about the ideas once Prewrite and Compose occur. As discussed in this chapter, there are many ways and reasons to select a particular experience. Seek out those potential moments in reading, science, social studies, and math. Or maximize the special events that you and your students experience throughout the year. What is essential is that the experience is *shared* by all students.

CHAPTER 4

Prewrite

Students must write in a variety of ways for real audiences and for real purposes. Prewrite is the place to ensure this happens. Consider these guiding questions: What is the purpose of the piece? What genre of writing will best support the purpose? Who will read this piece when it is finished?

As we described in Chapter 3, before the lesson ever began, the teacher intentionally chose the writing topic based on a shared classroom experience. After selecting what to write about, the next big decision is how to write about this experience. Thus, the teacher also considered the purpose and form of the writing, and she anticipated the audience who would read it. This is the essence of Prewrite.

As you will learn in this chapter, there are many ways that you can respond to an experience. You will determine the form and function of the piece ahead of time. Then, you and your students will begin planning the piece. You will notice that Prewrite expands and becomes more formal in the upper grades.

Responding to an Experience

A single experience can support multiple types of writing. For example, imagine that you have taken students on a field trip to a library. After the trip, you and your students can write about this experience in many ways, such as a thank-you note to the librarian, a how-to piece about checking out a book, a retell of the trip, an information piece on how libraries work, an advertisement persuading others to go to the library, or a chart listing what was learned. Looking at photos of interactive writing pieces can further illustrate this point.

As we mentioned in Chapter 3, a book read-aloud is a wonderful shared experience. After reading the text together, you and the students can respond to it in a variety of ways. For example, your class might retell the story, summarize the story, write a book review, or use the book's theme as a basis for an opinion paragraph. Table 3 shows how experiences can lead to many different Prewrite

WHAT TEACHERS ARE SAYING

Interactive writing actively involves the students by making them a part of the planning, constructing, and reading.

—Krystle (PreK)

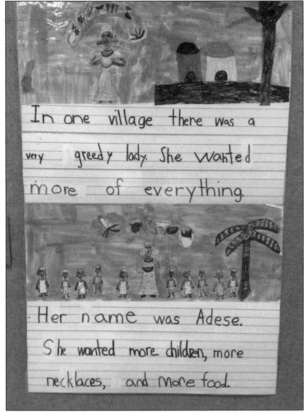

Retelling of African Fable (Grade 1)

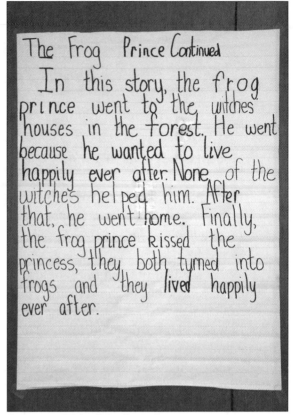

Summary of Fairy Tale (Grade 2)

In the book *Throw Your Tooth on the Roof*, Selby Beer wrote about unique tooth traditions from around the world. For example, in Mexico kids put their tooth in a box next to their bed, then a magic mouse comes and takes the tooth. It is a nonfiction book filled with interesting information.

Book Review (Grade 3)

Everlasting life is a major theme in the book *Tuck Everlasting* by Natalie Babbit. It would be a terrible situation to be a fifth grader forever. I would be embarrassed because I am stuck in fifth grade while my other friends moved along to the next grade. Also, I would not be able to get a driver's license, earn a college degree, and I would be stuck with the same bedtime forever. Moreover, not having children and being stuck on the "wheel of life" for an eternity would be dreadful! Being immortal would be abominable.

Opinion Paragraph (Grade 5)

Table 3 How to Connect an Experience to Multiple Types of Writing

Experience	Types of Writing
Field Trip to the Library	• Thank-you note/letter to librarian • How-to: How do you check out a book? • Retelling of the trip • Information piece: What did we learn on our trip? (e.g., How do libraries work? What do librarians do?) • Advertisement/persuasion: Why go to the library? • Opinion piece: Why are libraries important?
Math Content	• Definition of key concepts or principles (e.g., symmetry, equivalent fractions, odds and evens) • Description of a process (e.g., how to regroup, strategies for multistep problems, how to solve for an unknown variable) • Explanation of mathematical thinking (e.g., how we solved a word problem, how we figured out the solution)
Science Investigation	• Summary of key findings • Reflection on the process: What worked well? How might we change the investigation next time? How did the investigation confirm (or disconfirm) our initial thinking? • List or description of the procedure that was followed • Description of an observation made during the investigation • Claim based on what was found during the investigation with evidence to support the claim • Conclusion • List of new questions based on the investigation
Reading a Text	• New ending • Retelling of the story • Summary of the story or of the key information learned • Character analysis • Descriptive piece based on setting, events, or characters • Opinion piece using textual evidence: book review or critique • Similar piece that mirrors the author's craft or style
Holiday Celebration	• Information piece: What is the holiday? Why is it celebrated? • Compare and contrast piece: How is this holiday similar to or different from another? • Retelling of holiday event • Description of a holiday tradition • How-to: Write about how to complete a holiday activity (e.g. carving a pumpkin, writing a New Year's resolution, making a Valentine)

outcomes. Notice the ways that you and your students can write about a single experience!

Prewrite: The Architecture Behind Our Writing

Writing instruction is best when it both is meaningful for students and offers opportunities to write for different purposes (Graham & Harris, 2013; Morrow et al., 2011). Said another way, writers at *every age* can and should write for many reasons and for different audiences. They also need to learn about the ways we can write and how different writing genres serve distinct purposes. As we described in Chapter 2, the writing process begins with thoughtful planning.

During Prewrite, you work with students on these exact issues by discussing the purpose of the piece, considering the audience who will read it, and generating ideas to include. Prewrite focuses the writers and prepares them for Compose, and it models the importance of planning before writing.

For adult writers, issues around "form and function" are often fluid and overlap. For example, we often know the purpose for our writing ahead of time (e.g., a work proposal, an e-mail to a colleague, a welcome letter to students' parents). That said, as we plan our writing, we wonder about the best way to convey our ideas given the intended audience. Knowing both the purpose and the audience pushes us to have the appropriate organization and voice. This dynamic cycle of thinking is exactly what we model as we guide our students through Prewrite. To orchestrate this well in a classroom environment, multiple planning factors must be considered.

Planning for Prewrite

When interactive writing is used consistently over the course of the year, students stay engaged as a community of writers as they write on many topics and in many genres that are relevant to the curriculum. To effectively plan for this, you must know the following:

- Students' strengths as writers
- Students' areas for growth and development
- School's or district's curricular expectations for writing
- Real-world purposes for writing

Then, as you plan for Prewrite, you consider three important questions:

1. What will we be writing? (e.g., a letter, a list, a summary, a description)
2. Why are we writing this? (e.g., to inform, to explain, to entertain, to persuade, to teach, to give thanks, to reflect)

3. Who will read this writing piece? (e.g., our peers, adults in our school, our teacher, a person in the community, ourselves)

As you will see, most decisions made during Prewrite are planned ahead of time by the teacher.

What Writers Need

As teachers, you frequently notice your students' writing in both formal and informal ways. At key moments in the year (beginning, middle, or end) you might have students respond to a prompt or choose a piece of writing from their collection of work to assess their progress. You might also look through their writing folders or notebooks each week and record specific areas of strength and areas needing more support. Or you might informally review student journals, science notebooks, or other short written responses from other subject areas. Because of this, you have a good sense of what students need in order to grow and develop as independent writers. As you plan your Prewrite, always keep students in mind. The teaching you do during Prewrite needs to support their "just right" writing needs.

During the actual Prewrite phase of the lesson, you skillfully lead a conversation with your students around the plan for the piece. Embedded in this discussion are the essential issues any writer considers related to purpose, genre, and audience. The three questions from earlier can inform your teaching language. Even though the Prewrite plan was decided by you ahead of time, the conversation will feel collaborative as students are encouraged to think about how they will contribute their ideas for the piece.

Curriculum Expectations

In addition to knowing your students, you often know in advance what kinds of pieces they must write in your particular grade over the course of the year. This guidance may come from state or district standards or be found in your school's curriculum. Having this information allows you to strategically select the optimum genre for each interactive writing piece you create with students. When determining the form the writing will take, consider the following:

- The types of writing your students need to know and understand over the school year
- The specific features of a genre that you need to teach students
- Matching the ideas/topics from Experience with an appropriate genre
- Where you are in the school year (beginning, middle, or end)
- Unit goals (final projects or assessment expectations)

- The types of writing your students have completed already this year
- The types of writing your students have not yet tried this year

The Power of Real-World Purpose

As these earlier points are taken into account, you also must think about the purpose the writing holds beyond your curriculum or standards. Remember, in the world outside of school, adults write every day for real-world purposes. They write to inform, explain, persuade, learn more, or entertain. For students, the real-world importance that writing holds can sometimes be lost if they write only for teachers, grades, stickers, or stars. Writing *instruction* is most powerful when it is linked with real audiences and real purposes (Graham & Harris, 2013). Fortunately, interactive writing requires you to select *genuine* ways for students to share their writing. During your Prewrite planning, you address this authenticity by considering the following:

- The purpose of the piece (to inform, entertain, persuade, or explain)
- The real person/people who will read the piece or benefit from the piece (e.g., students and adults within your school, students and adults in other schools, family, community leaders, authors)
- How the piece might extend beyond your interactive writing lesson
- The place the writing might go (e.g., your classroom walls, a letter sent locally or far away, a blog posted on a website)

To sum up, planning before we write is an essential step in the writing process that we want students to know and understand. During Prewrite, we guide students in how to do this. There are three big ideas we keep in mind. First, we let our students know that we write for many purposes and that knowing about different genres helps us pick the best way to convey our message. Second, the audience for our writing influences how we write. Third, we keep both the purpose for writing *and* the audience in mind when we plan our piece. With these essential ideas in mind, we now explore how Prewrite adjusts and expands through the grades.

Looking at Prewrite Through the Grades

As writers grow and develop, it follows that their needs do the same. Thus, the Prewrite phase evolves as the writing becomes longer and more complex. As you will notice, the essential pieces of Prewrite (purpose, genre, and audience) will be present at all grade levels. What changes is how the ideas for the piece are more formally generated, organized, and captured in writing using several best practice prewriting structures, including brainstorming and graphic organizers (Graham & Harris, 2013).

Prewrite: PreK–2

From the beginning, young writers need to know that they can write for many reasons. They need to be clear about their audience and that the format in which they write changes to fit their purpose. For example, kindergartners can write a to-do list to *remind* themselves how to prepare for the class show. First graders can write a letter to *thank* the firefighters who visited their school (refer to the example on **p. 39** in Chapter 3).

For emergent writers, the Prewrite step most often involves you deciding on the purpose and form for writing and telling students at the beginning of the lesson why they are writing the piece, as well as clarifying for students who the audience will be. Throughout this chapter, we have included a series of authentic teaching moments that allow you to "Listen in on a Lesson." These excerpts from real lessons highlight genuine teacher–student interactions.

The first lesson features Heather working with her kindergartners during Prewrite. Keep in mind that Heather knew before she sat down at the easel that her students would write a to-do list.

LISTEN IN ON A LESSON: Kindergarten

Heather says to her class:

> We have so much to do to get ready for our class assembly this Friday. Do you know what I do when I want to remind myself of things I don't want to forget? I write myself a note or a to-do list. A to-do list is a list of all the things you need to do. I write a few words to remind myself so I do not forget anything. I usually number them so I can check off my list when I do each thing. Today we are going to make a to-do list for ourselves so we can remember some really important things we absolutely must do to be ready to perform at the end of this week.

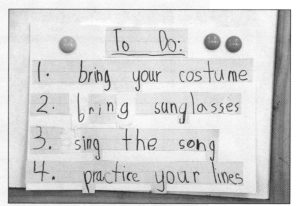

To-Do List for Performance (Kindergarten)

In the second lesson, Katie introduces the interactive writing project to her first graders by explaining that they will retell a favorite story after having read many versions of the tale "The Three Little Pigs." From the beginning, these young students understood they would spend multiple interactive writing lessons putting the story in their own words to share with peers.

Katie says to her class:

We have had such fun reading 20 different versions of "The Three Little Pigs"!
We have read traditional ones and funny ones and ones in which the author changed
the setting or storyteller to make them original. For the next two weeks, we will write
our own version of this story. We need to make sure our story has a strong beginning,

Excerpts From a Retell of "The Three Little Pigs" (Grade 1)

middle, and end and uses some of our favorite folk-tale language. We will write one page each day. Then we will turn this story into a beautiful big book that we can hang on the bulletin board outside of our class so everyone in the school can read it when they walk by our room.

The Prewrite stage in an early elementary classroom is most often short and simple and flows quickly into Compose. However, its purpose of setting up a thoughtful lesson is invaluable.

Prewrite: Grades 2–5

Instructional decisions for older writers require thoughtful planning, and it may look different depending on your goals for the interactive writing piece. It can be more or less formal, shorter or longer, and may or may not include note-taking and graphic organizers to capture initial ideas and plans. In all cases, the Prewrite discussion informs the writing piece. Thus it follows that any charts or organizers created during Prewrite are directly tied to the writing you and your students will do during Compose and Share the Pen.

If the goal of the interactive writing lesson is a single sentence, then it follows that the time and work within Prewrite may be shorter and perhaps less formal. If, however, the final piece of interactive writing is longer or is something that may take several days to complete, it may be that the Prewrite is

COMPARE & CONTRAST
• When we <u>compare</u> we: look at two different things and see what they have in common
• When we <u>contrast</u> we: look at the differences
• Look for clues that tell you if the author is COMPARING or CONTRASTING two or more things

CLUE WORDS

<u>COMPARE</u>	<u>CONTRAST</u>
alike	different
both	however
same	unlike
have in common	than
similar	while

Prewrite Graphic Organizer Focused on the Characteristics of Writing a Compare and Contrast Piece (Grade 3)

longer and is informed by anchor charts that provide details about the genre or vocabulary word banks. Sometimes the charts and organizers are prepared ahead of time by you. Other times, the charts are built together along with your students.

During Prewrite, you—the teacher—are doing the actual writing. Sharing the pen or keyboard comes later in the lesson. As always, the interactive writing method models what real writers do when they write for different purposes and audiences. Sometimes an extensive Prewrite is needed and sometimes a short plan suffices.

The "Listen in on a Lesson" scenarios for grades 4 and 5 show how Prewrite flows in the upper grades.

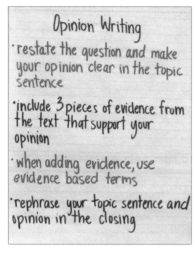

Opinion Writing

- restate the question and make your opinion clear in the topic sentence

- include 3 pieces of evidence from the text that support your opinion

- when adding evidence, use evidence based terms

- rephrase your topic sentence and opinion in the closing

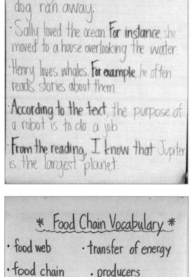

Evidence Based Terms:

- The boy was sad because his dog ran away.
- Sally loved the ocean. For instance, she moved to a house overlooking the water.
- Henry loves whales. For example, he often reads stories about them
- According to the text, the purpose of a robot is to do a job
- From the reading, I know that Jupiter is the largest planet.

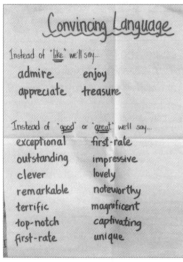

Convincing Language

Instead of "like" we'll say...

admire   enjoy
appreciate   treasure

Instead of "good" or "great" we'll say...

exceptional   first-rate
outstanding   impressive
clever   lovely
remarkable   noteworthy
terrific   magnificent
top-notch   captivating
first-rate   unique

* Food Chain Vocabulary *

- food web   · transfer of energy
- food chain   · producers
- consumers   · decomposers
- scavengers   · omnivore
- carnivore   · herbivore
- ecosystem   · primary consumer
- secondary consumer

Examples of Prewrite Anchor Charts (Grades 3–5)

Jennifer worked with fourth-grade students who were struggling with how to end their pieces well. She approached the Prewrite with efficiency by doing three things:

1. *Named the goal for the lesson*—to practice writing a stronger conclusion sentence that enlightens readers about the topic

2. *Told students why a strong conclusion was essential*—to fully end the piece in a satisfying and thoughtful way for the audience

3. *Selected the form the interactive writing would take*—a sample piece of writing that her students had written together in an earlier lesson; they would *rewrite only the last sentence* in order to practice the craft of closure

---

LISTEN IN ON A LESSON: Grade 4

Jennifer says to her class:

> *I know from reading your pieces and from conferring with some of you that many writers in our class are having a hard time when it comes to endings. This is something that all writers go through—finding the best way to end their piece. The conclusion is the last thing our audience reads, so it's a very important part of our piece. Here are two thoughtful ideas to keep in mind about writing a strong conclusion.*

Jennifer shows students an anchor chart titled "Strong Endings" and reads it aloud:

1. Strong endings satisfy readers.

2. Strong endings enlighten readers one last time about the topic.

The word enlighten *is a strong verb. It means to teach or to inform—but in a convincing way. So a strong ending will satisfy readers and will teach them one last idea about the topic—in a meaningful or convincing way.*

Today we are going to work on this idea of a strong ending using the book recommendation we wrote together last week about Bud, Not Buddy. *We will look only at the concluding sentence—how we ended the piece.*

Notice we ended it by writing the sentences, "It is a really great book. You should read it!"

Hmm. I'm wondering if that really meets the standard for a strong ending. I'm not convinced that it enlightens our readers about Bud, Not Buddy. *We are going to think about this together, and then we'll rewrite a concluding sentence (or two) that we all agree does two things: (1) satisfies readers and (2) enlightens readers one last time about the book* Bud, Not Buddy.

Original Ending: "It is a really great book. You should read it!"

Revised Ending: "It is an action-packed book that will teach you about an important time in American history, jazz music, and the importance of family. You should definitely read it!"

In this Prewrite, it took less than 10 minutes for Jennifer to engage the students, establish the goal and purpose for the writing, and share the best format (i.e., two sentences).

There are other times when Prewrite may merit more formal time and guidance. When Joan was working in Atara's fifth-grade classroom, students were in the midst of a unit on how to write effective opinions. The culminating project of the unit required students to write a multiparagraph opinion essay. With this in mind, Atara and Joan used their class novel, *Tuck Everlasting* (Babbit, 1975), as the shared experience for an interactive writing piece focused on point of view. Students first discussed and debated the pros and cons of living forever as a fifth grader. Then they wrote an opinion paragraph from one of these perspectives. (Refer to the completed opinion paragraph on **page 44**.)

During Prewrite, Joan did four things:

1. *Named the goal for the lesson*—to practice writing a piece that supports a point of view using reasons and information

2. *Told students why points of view matter within the context of opinion writing*—when writing an opinion, having logically ordered reasons and information to support your point of view is essential

3. *Selected the form the interactive writing would take*—the students would "take a stand" and write a paragraph for or against being a fifth grader forever

4. *Identified the real-world purpose the writing would hold*—the interactive writing piece would be an exemplar students would return to when they wrote their own opinion piece later on in the unit

---

LISTEN IN ON A LESSON: *Grade 5*

Joan says to Atara's students:

> *In the next few weeks, you will be writing a letter to your principal about whether year-round school is a good idea. You will need to "take a stand" on this issue and try to convince Ms. Anderson that your point of view is the right one. When you write a piece like this, you need to express your opinion clearly and have reasons to support it that make sense. It is not enough to say, "Because that's what I think." You need solid information to back up your opinion.*
>
> *In order to prepare you for writing your upcoming letter to Ms. Anderson, we will work together on an opinion piece that considers another interesting topic. We will take a stand on an issue and give solid reasons that back up our opinion. You will be able to use our finished piece as an example for your letter to Ms. Anderson.*
>
> *You recently finished the novel* Tuck Everlasting *by Natalie Babbit. That story considers a very intriguing topic—the idea of living forever, of everlasting life! In the novel, the characters consider both the good and bad parts of everlasting life. Different characters had different opinions on this. Tuck felt one way, for sure. Jesse had other thoughts. Take a moment to turn and talk with the people at your table about the different views of everlasting life that played out in* Tuck Everlasting.

Students talk for two minutes at their tables.

> *I heard some thoughtful points discussed in your conversations. Keep those in mind as we consider the plan for our piece. We will take a stand on this question: Is living forever as a fifth grader a good idea? Let's think about that idea for just a moment in silence. Would YOU want to live forever as a fifth grader?*

The room is silent for 30 seconds while students consider this idea on their own.

> *I'm sure that you each have some thoughts and opinions on this topic. Because you ARE fifth graders, you know the good parts and the not-so-good parts better than most people! Before we write an opinion piece, let's consider both sides of this issue. Once we have considered both sides, we will take a stand and then write a paragraph that gives our opinion and supports it with reasons and information that make sense.*

Joan shows the students a blank T-Chart on the screen.

I have made a T-Chart for us to organize our ideas. Just like in the text, there are different points of view that we need to consider. There are some good parts about being a fifth grader forever—we call those the "Pros"—and there are the negative parts of being a fifth grader forever—we call those the "Cons." Take three minutes to discuss at your table the pros of being a fifth grader forever. Talk only about the positive aspects of being your age and in your grade forever. Turn and talk about this!

Students engage in lively discussion for three minutes.

You had a LOT to say about the benefits of staying a fifth grader forever. Let's share out those ideas, and I'll type them into our graphic organizer.

Students share the "Pros" of living forever as a fifth grader. Joan records these ideas on the document. The students follow the same discussion protocol for the "Cons," and then those ideas are shared out and recorded by Joan on the other side of the T-Chart.

Now that we have captured your ideas about this topic, we need to take a stand on the issue. Will we say that living forever as a fifth grader is a good thing or bad thing? Which side should we take?

After a brief discussion, Joan made the final decision in the moment on the basis of the ideas that were generated during Prewrite. Their opinion piece would assert that living forever as a fifth grader would *not* be a good idea.

Now that we have taken a stand on the issue, we can begin to write. Tomorrow, we'll use our Prewrite ideas as we build our first sentence.

In this case, Prewrite was its own 30-minute lesson. The introductory steps of Prewrite, the depth of student discussions, and the recording of ideas onto a pros-and-cons graphic organizer required this amount of time. Students had much to say about the topic; thus, the written notes and ideas typed up by the teacher prevented anything from being forgotten.

Table 4 provides a list of helpful Prewrite strategies and graphic organizers that

Living Forever as a Fifth Grader: Pros and Cons	
Pros	Cons
<ul><li>more time for playing</li><li>get to play sports for a long time</li><li>don't need to pay bills</li><li>won't need to get a full time job</li><li>people will think you are really smart (because you have learned everything already)</li><li>get more Christmas presents when you are a kid</li><li>if you have a nice teacher, you will have him/her more than once</li></ul>	<ul><li>stuck in fifth grade while your friends move on into middle school</li><li>not able to go on to high school or college</li><li>can't become an engineer or architect</li><li>stuck with the same bedtime</li><li>can't get a driver's license</li><li>have to learn the same things over and over again in school</li><li>not able to have children; can't pass your spirit on to the next generation</li><li>not able to get to the "afterlife" or heaven</li><li>"stuck" on the wheel of life</li></ul>

Completed Graphic Organizer From Whole-Class Brainstorming for an Opinion Paragraph (Grade 5)

Table 4 Helpful Tools and Organizers for Prewrite

Tool or Organizer	Works Well for...
Two-Columned Chart (T-chart)	• Showing two points of view (pros/cons), cause and effect, problem and solution, thesis ideas and textual evidence, etc.
Brainstorm/List	• Generating many ideas quickly • Jotting down key words/phrases • Modeling that full sentences are not always needed when you are planning for writing
Web	• Descriptive writing • Character analysis • Showing relationships
Venn Diagram	• Compare/Contrast • Similarities/Differences
Anchor Chart	• Highlighting important features of a genre • Listing helpful vocabulary words or key phrases • Writing down reminders of what to include in the piece
Flowchart	• How To's • Sequence • Investigations/Processes
Multiparagraph Essay Organizers (variety of styles)	• Planning out ideas for each paragraph (thesis, reasons, evidence, etc.) • Highlighting introductions and conclusions • Collecting evidence from sources/texts, etc.

upper-grade teachers may opt to use during a more formal Prewrite. These organizers serve multiple purposes: They allow students to plan and generate ideas strategically, and they also allow students to understand better how prewriting tools and organizers work. Any charts or organizers that are created during Prewrite will be used again as references for ideas and language when students move into Compose and Share the Pen.

In our ever-demanding teaching schedules, time is always factor. Working through an extended Prewrite certainly takes more time. However, there will be instructional moments when this prewriting work is time well spent. Even so, we do not recommend extended Prewrites for *every* interactive writing lesson in grades 2–5. Rather, we recommend that you use the following questions to guide your Prewrite decisions:

- What type of writing will we work on during these lessons? (e.g., response to literature, science investigation, mathematical procedure)
- What content area will this writing support? English language arts? Science? Social studies? Math?

- What will the final interactive writing piece be? A sentence? Two sentences? A paragraph? A multiparagraph piece?

- What elements of craft and conventions do I anticipate highlighting? What exact planning does this piece need? How much time does this require?

- How do I envision the interactive writing piece being helpful beyond the lesson itself? Is this a one-time practice opportunity, or will students come back to this piece again?

- Will a more formal Prewrite strengthen the interactive writing piece?

- How have I approached Prewrite in past interactive writing sessions? Am I doing too many short Prewrites? Would a longer Prewrite session be helpful for students?

Final Thoughts

A well-planned Prewrite is essential in interactive writing. Selecting the most appropriate writing purpose, genre, and audience for students is a powerful teaching decision. It requires that you know your students, your grade level's writing expectations, and the real-world purposes the writing can hold. Prewrite will look and sound different across the grades. In grades PreK–2, it is typically brief and flows quickly into Compose. In grades 3–5, it often expands and includes more formal planning. The overarching goal is for all students to understand that writing serves many functions and that the format must fit the purpose for writing.

The teaching work done in Prewrite strategically informs you and your students as you work through Compose, where craft becomes paramount. In our next chapter, we show you how this happens.

CHAPTER 5

Compose

Compose is the heart of the interactive writing lesson. As you facilitate rich conversations with your students, you teach them about the craft of writing. Consider these questions as you move through this step: What are the qualities of writing that make up craft? What language and teaching moves support the discussions around craft? How do we plan and prepare for Compose?

During the Compose phase of an interactive writing lesson, the teacher and students discuss the specific content of the writing. Students share their ideas as the teacher helps them negotiate the precise language of the text to be written. The teacher provides instruction to support students' writing development by synthesizing the ideas she hears from students, proposing vocabulary or language that will advance the ideas, and, in some cases, ultimately suggesting the "final sentence" based on their discussion. The teacher might also use think-alouds to model for students why that sentence is most appropriate.

A novice observer might describe Compose as a natural conversation about writing facilitated by the teacher and filled with lively student input. Although this is the case, there is much more happening in these moments. The *teaching* within Compose is instructionally rich and multifaceted (Roth, 2009). Moreover, it is informed both by characteristics of good writing and by students' independent writing. It honors and strengthens their current understandings of language and literacy. As you will discover in this chapter, Compose is a critical piece of an interactive writing lesson.

WHAT TEACHERS ARE SAYING

I enjoy how interactive writing offers strong support for struggling writers to compose a text that they can read fluently, giving them the confidence to try out the same strategies in their independent writing.

—Heather M. (Kindergarten)

Compose: A Collaborative Conversation About Craft

During Compose, you work with your students on drafting and revising as you determine the precise language of the text that will be written that day. Most often, you build a single sentence at a time, although the length and complexity grows and expands as writers develop. Compose is best characterized as a collaborative conversation with students about the *craft* of writing. Let's first talk more about what we mean when we say "craft."

The Craft of Writing

Skilled writers are strategic, motivated, and knowledgeable about the *craft* of writing (Hayes, 1996). Think for a moment about a favorite book you have read recently or from years ago. Think about the book's qualities or characteristics that you enjoyed or appreciated. Perhaps the writer used creative, flowing sentences like Sandra Cisneros's *The House on Mango Street* or Barbara Kingsolver's *The Poisonwood Bible*. Perhaps the engaging ideas and masterful organization of the story kept you hanging on every word like in *The Firm* by John Grisham or in one of J. K. Rowling's Harry Potter books. Or when reading a nonfiction text, such as *Unbroken* by Laura Hillenbrand or Ron Suskind's *A Hope in the Unseen*, you savored the author's words and voice as they described unfamiliar events, making them come alive for you. These are the qualities of craft—the heart and soul of writing.

Much has been written about how to approach the craft of writing with our students (Culham, 2003; Culham, 2005; Pinnell & Fountas, 2011; Spandel, 2013). When we think about teaching craft during interactive writing, we focus on ideas, organization, word choice, sentence fluency, and voice. Though these qualities of writing are distinct, they often overlap during the Compose phase of the lesson. As you and your students construct a sentence in "real time," the teaching of craft unfolds in these unscripted moments.

Ideas and Organization

When we think about ideas, we focus on the meaning and message of our writing (Spandel, 2013). Knowing our topic well and being able to describe both the main points and important details are the essence of ideas. Because of the shared experience that informs interactive writing, much of the work around ideas has been considered before the Compose phase begins. However, during Compose you guide your students to incorporate and organize their ideas clearly into the piece. You help them keep the ideas focused and emphasize that writing needs to make sense to the readers. Sequencing ideas receives considerable attention for writers of all ages. Students benefit when you show them how to convey a sense of order by using specific words in their writing and by making sure there is a logical flow of ideas from one sentence to the next.

WHAT TEACHERS ARE SAYING

I especially like generating ideas for what we want to say with our words. Kids are throwing out ideas, and they are building upon each other's thoughts, hands start waving, they are getting excited and immersed in the writing process.   —Cassandra (Kindergarten)

Word Choice

As writers, we strive to choose the precise words and phrases that will allow our audience to fully understand our ideas. We also work to be creative in our choices and to include interesting vocabulary so our readers will stay engaged. As you build a sentence with students, talk with them about these word choice decisions. Guide them to choose words that show rather than tell and that allow readers to form vivid images in their mind. You also use this opportunity to introduce more complex vocabulary in a meaningful context that is then immediately applied to their collaborative writing.

You can use the Compose phase to show your students how to avoid overused words such as *fun, nice, sad,* or *like* by pausing and thinking aloud with them about other, more compelling choices such as *fantastic, heartwarming, disappointed,* or *appreciate*. You might also urge students to be precise with their words by using specific details. For example, refine an initial sentence such as "We ate a good snack" into a precise, interesting sentence such as "We ate juicy apple slices." The teaching emphasis here is that writers choose their words carefully so that the audience can fully understand their piece.

Language and Sentence Fluency

As you teach your students to develop and organize their ideas and to consider word choice, you also coach them in the flow of their language to work on sentence fluency. Culham (2005) describes sentence fluency as "the auditory trait, where (children) learn to read with (their) ears right along with (their) eyes" (p. 207). Sentence fluency is both the grammar that makes a group of words a sentence and the way the sentences sound to the ear (Culham, 2005).

Throughout the Compose phase, you can have students repeat their sentence aloud before writing it down to "make sure it sounds right to their ears." You also encourage sentence variety and draw students' attention to how each sentence begins differently and is a different length. Ultimately sentences are crafted to have a pleasing sound and interesting cadence.

Voice

Spandel (2013) tells us that voice is the "heartbeat of the writer" (p. 129). It is the unique quality that propels a piece far beyond just words on a page. Readers connect with a text when they "hear" the author's passions, convictions, authority, or sense of humor. When we use voice in our writing, we put our "fingerprints on the page" (p. 129). As you work through Compose, students will suggest words and phrases that allow you to tap this aspect of writing. When you hear their passion or enthusiasm or catch a moment of their wit or humor, you have an opportunity to notice and name the power of voice. As you write for different purposes and audiences, you talk with your students about how the voice within the writing will adjust as needed. Understanding this nuance is important for developing writers.

Teaching for Craft During Compose

The conversation around craft that evolves during Compose is enriched as you prompt students to say more, reach for more interesting vocabulary, use their unique voices, or extend their ideas. The interactions are scaffolded by *you*: the expert writer in the room who best knows the needs of these student writers and who can help advance their understanding of craft.

As you select students to talk and respond during the Compose phase, one may give an initial thought or idea while another might offer a complete sentence. Hearing from only one student is not enough. Instead, multiple ideas are considered and evaluated. This back-and-forth mediation occurs in a supportive way as students are encouraged to try out new words and phrases or to speak using the language required for written text. Together, you continue to work your way through the writing process as you draft and revise your message.

You will learn quickly that these discussions offer multiple insights into students' current language and literacy capacities. You hear what students know and understand about the topic as they talk. You also listen in for vocabulary, sentence structure, and fluency. As you take in this information, you are identifying quickly the golden teaching opportunities where you might propel student learning about language and literacy. Your role is to be the skilled facilitator, which means you pull together the many ideas from your students or take their incomplete thoughts and model for them how to refine and revise them in the moment. The end result is a well-crafted sentence.

As you negotiate these conversations strategically to build off your students' strengths and to advance your students as writers, you provide dynamic *differentiated* instruction within this *whole-group* lesson (Roth, 2009). You are propelling your students just beyond what they are able to do on their own by supporting and refining their input (Pearson & Gallagher, 1983; Vygotsky, 1978).

WHAT TEACHERS ARE SAYING

I like that it exposes the class in a whole-group setting to actively participate in the thought process and work process of forming sentences.

—Mollie (Grade 1)

Compose: Why Bother?

After selecting a meaningful shared experience and working through Prewrite with your students, "cutting to the chase" might be tempting. By this we mean sometimes teachers want to move quickly into the actual writing and opt to determine the sentence or paragraph to be written without student input. This may be a time-saver in the short run; however, the long-term benefits gained from a robust Compose discussion cannot be understated. Following are four reasons why Compose is valuable and why it must be included authentically in every interactive writing lesson.

Focus on Craft

Meaning is considered throughout all steps in an interactive writing lesson; however, during Compose you focus *exclusively* on the craft of writing while you construct a sentence (Roth, 2009). In other parts of the lesson (e.g., Share the Pen, Review), attention will be paid to the details of each letter or word, including spelling. Time also will be spent on letter formation, handwriting, spacing, and punctuation. Compose is the one place where you highlight for your students how to organize ideas, choose words intentionally, create interesting sentences, and capture their unique voices.

Let's be clear here: The craft of writing requires deep and complex thinking. Students need to know and understand how to approach and wrestle with craft in order to develop and expand their own writing capacities. Compose is the time within an interactive writing lesson to support your students with these essential processes and skills.

Bridge Oral Language to Written Text

Compose is the place to highlight for students how talk and written text are sometimes different. In our literacy coaching work, we often hear teachers remark that their students "write like they talk" or "have a lot to say but can't put it into writing." As adults, we know how our casual talk with friends differs from more formal professional conversations. We also know how a quick text or e-mail compares with a formal letter required for work. These sophisticated understandings need to be taught explicitly to our developing writers. For example, in a simple phrase, you model how to switch their informal talk into Standard English text by saying something like, "I hear what you are saying. When we write it, we say it like this...."

Students begin to recognize that their talk and writing are connected. You continue to guide them to this realization as you affirm their spoken language and model for them how to turn their talk into written words. Eventually, they will begin to recognize the changes they need to make and will make them more quickly on their own. The Compose phase is an optimum place to reinforce this issue of syntax.

Magnify Draft and Revise

As we described in Chapter 2, the writing process is not lock-step. It is fluid and dynamic for each writer and for each piece of writing. During Compose, you slow down the writing process in order to magnify what it means to draft and revise ideas. As you and your students discuss the sentence to be written, you initiate new ideas and then evaluate and refine them. This thinking occurs in the moment as needed. This is what it means to draft and revise. It is the real work that writers do—and it is hard. The Compose phase allows students to practice this with your support.

Give Students Ownership of the Writing

Throughout an interactive writing lesson, students are participating in an authentic and meaningful writing activity. In addition, they are working together to solve problems they will face when they write independently (Brotherton & Williams, 2002). There are moments when you direct the learning, and there are moments for individual students to take the lead. There are also times when students turn and talk with a nearby peer to give more voices a chance to be heard. As these conversations evolve, students become more invested, engaged, and supported in how to compose a meaningful text. They offer their ideas and consider the ideas of others.

> **WHAT TEACHERS ARE SAYING**
>
> As students build the sentence, they bounce ideas off each other. They put their heads together and think together. I like listening to their thinking. —Melissa (Grade 5)

When the sentence composing is complete, all of your students feel authorship of what text will be written. *Their* thoughts will go on the paper. By co-constructing each sentence for the interactive writing piece, students solidify and revise their thinking of *how* to build strong sentences. This is the key takeaway that ultimately will affect their independent writing. Compose facilitates student ownership of both the writing process and the writing product.

If you skip Compose and choose the sentence for your students to write, you eliminate valuable opportunities for them to think about the craft of writing. You also take away guided instruction within a safe practice environment where students can consider how spoken language translates into written text. Compose offers a powerful place in which students can practice what it means to draft and revise. Moreover, if the sentence is given to them, students will not see themselves as capable authors. The Compose step builds their confidence and deepens their engagement.

The Language and Sequence of Compose

Compose should feel like a natural conversation with your students, and you should bring your teaching style and voice to the discussion. That said, there is a general flow to this part of the lesson, and there are some guiding phrases and questions to use with students that will help facilitate a productive discussion. Table 5 provides the sequence of Compose along with suggestions for teacher language.

Table 5 The Language and Sequence of Compose

Teaching Steps Within Compose	Possible Teaching Language
Transition From Prewrite Into Compose	• Remember, today we are writing a [insert the writing type/genre] for [insert intended purpose and/or audience]. • Our goal for our writing is…. • Let's start by rereading what we have written.
Initiate Sentence Building (Draft)	• How can we say this in a sentence? • How might we write this? • What words would we say? • What comes next? (if continuing from writing on a previous day)
Prompt and Negotiate Discussion (Draft and Revise)	• Does someone else have another idea of how we might say this? • Can someone add to the sentence? • How can we take those ideas and put them together in one sentence? • Listen as I say the sentence aloud. What do you think? Is that saying what we want it to say? • Does our sentence sound clear? • Let's make sure this makes sense with our last sentence. • Should we start our sentence differently from the last one? • Will [insert audience] be able to understand it if we say it this way? • Is there another word we can use to make our sentence clearer? • Does this sound right? • [Propose two sentences] Which one sounds better to you? • Does it say what we want it to say? • Have we used the best words for our audience? • I like the way we… [describe the craft element that students incorporated successfully].
Wrap-Up	• Our sentence is complete. • We're ready to write down our sentence. • Let's say our sentence together one more time (a few times) before we write. • We included all the essential points in our sentence.

Part 1: Transition From Prewrite

Composing begins in two ways. If this is a new piece, quickly refer back to the Prewrite conversations and then transition students into the actual sentence building. If this is a piece that was started in a previous session, you do two things: (1) remind students of the overall purpose and goal for the writing and (2) reread aloud everything that has been written thus far. This second step models what real writers do when they sit down to write: They reread their earlier work. This is an important skill for your students to learn and apply in their own independent writing.

Part 2: Initiate Sentence Building (Draft)

After the initial setup, you move into sentence building with students by asking something like, "How can we say this in a sentence?" or "How might we write this? What words would we say?" If your sentence is a continuation from the previous one, you might simply begin with "What comes next?"

Part 3: Prompt and Negotiate Discussion (Draft and Revise)

As students begin sharing their ideas for the sentence, your role remains important yet becomes nuanced. Remember, your role is to lift the quality of language and voice while honoring the words and phrases students suggest. You prompt student thinking, advance the discussion, and evaluate the quality of the sentence by saying things like the following:

- Does someone else have another idea of how we might say this?
- Can someone add on to the sentence?
- How can we take those ideas and put them together in one sentence?
- Listen as I say the sentence aloud. What do you think? Is that saying what we want it to say?
- Does our sentence sound clear?
- Let's make sure this makes sense with our last sentence.
- Should we start our sentence differently from the last one?
- Will [insert audience] be able to understand it if we say it this way?
- Is there another word we can use to make our sentence more clear?
- Does this sound right?
- [Propose two sentences] Which one sounds better to you?
- Does it say what we want it to say?
- Did we use the best words for our audience?

You can use think-alouds and articulate for students why a sentence is a strong one by saying something like, "I like the way we started this sentence differently from the last one and combined two ideas into one sentence."

Part 4: Wrap-Up

When you and your students have reached consensus on the sentence to be written, the Compose step is complete. This means the ideas, organization, words, and sentence structure are in place. You will need to remember the exact language of the sentence as you and your students move into Share the Pen, where you actually transcribe the sentence onto paper or screen. There are many ways to do this. You might opt to have students repeat it aloud several times, whisper the sentence to a friend, or clap out the words. Alternatively, you might write the sentence on a small sticky note. Table 6 includes a list of additional ideas.

As you will notice, some of the strategies for remembering the sentence support classroom management issues (e.g., students who need a break from sitting on the carpet will enjoy standing up and clapping for each word) while other strategies are setting the stage for Share the Pen or Keyboard (e.g., tapping the words onto the page to show where they will be written down or asking students to close their eyes and visualize the words of the sentence). Being creative with students helps them stay engaged in the lesson so try out different ways and use the strategies that work best.

The repeated experience with the sentence is an intentional teaching move to help you and your students remember the sentence. The repetition

Table 6 Engaging Ways to Practice and Remember the Sentence

Grade Levels	Ways to Remember and Practice the Sentence
PreK–2	• Whole class says it together in different ways (e.g., regular voices, whispers, deep voice) • Different groups of students repeat the sentence (e.g., just boys, just girls, the right side of the carpet) • Students turn and tell their neighbor the sentence • Students clap or snap the sentence (each word gets a clap or snap) • Students say the sentence with physical movements (e.g., twist for each word, jump for each word) • Students count the number of words as they repeat the sentence aloud with you • You tap where the words will be written on the paper as students say the sentence
2–5	• Students say and repeat the sentence two or three times as a whole class • Students use partners to practice the sentence; each partner repeats the sentence while the other partner listens for fluency and accuracy • Students say the sentence in their heads and count the number of words • Students close their eyes as you say the sentence and they visualize the words • You have students repeat the sentence slowly while you jot it down on paper or a sticky note

also makes rereading easier. The sentence becomes familiar and helps students improve their oral language as they internalize new vocabulary and sentence structures.

Ongoing: Connect to Students' Independent Writing

The ultimate goal of interactive writing lessons is to improve students' independent writing. In addition to helping students thoughtfully write the best sentence for this specific piece, you want to make explicit connections between what they are learning in this lesson and what they are expected to do independently.

For example, after working through exactly how to express ideas, you can say, "Sometimes it takes a couple of tries to figure out how you want to say something, even when you are by yourself. You have to stop and think about how to put your thoughts together to make sense." Or if you tried out several words before choosing the best one, you could say, "Notice how we just took time to try out several words. You should do that in your own writing too. You do not always need to write the first word that comes to mind. Take time to choose the best word." Don't leave it to chance that students will apply what they are learning in a group session to their own work (Darling-Hammond & Austin, 2003). Instead, you want to be clear about how they can use what they are learning.

How Compose Changes Over Time

Although the essential components of an interactive writing lesson stay the same throughout the elementary grades, there are several key shifts to consider as writers become more fluent and mature. One is that the lesson sequence becomes more fluid and dynamic. In the primary grades, the interactive writing lesson format is linear. Because of the age and skill of the readers and writers, the class usually writes one sentence each time as the actual writing is slower and they benefit most from simple texts.

For the primary grades, the progression from Compose to Share the Pen to Review is direct. You agree on one sentence during Compose and then write it during Share the Pen. You and the students revise and edit your writing as you go and then move into Review of your work when the sentence is complete. Although your class often spends several days working to complete an entire piece, typically you complete a single sentence during each interactive writing lesson. Therefore, there is only one Compose.

Once students become more fluent writers, there is more flow between Compose and Share the Pen. Depending on your goals, time frame, and the skill of the writers, the class might write several sentences or whole paragraphs in one interactive writing lesson. To do this, the class would move back and forth between the composing and constructing phases. You would negotiate the precise message sentence by sentence, as explained in this chapter, and then share the pen after each sentence is decided. Then you compose and then write again.

Listening in on some lessons will help illustrate the nuances of the Compose phase and how these discussions change and develop as writers mature. In the first Listen in on a Lesson, you will hear Heather work with her kindergartners to write a book about leaves they collected on a recent walk to a local park.

LISTEN IN ON A LESSON: Kindergarten

Experience

The kindergartners collected leaves on a visit to a local park as part of a science unit on autumn and trees.

Prewrite

The students planned to write a book about leaves that they would share with other students and visitors to their classroom.

Compose

Part 1: Transition Into Compose

Heather: Today we are going to continue writing our book about leaves so everyone who visits our class can read about our collection. What do writers do before they start writing?

Class: Read!

Heather: Yes, we always reread what we did yesterday and the day before yesterday to remind us what we have written. Let's do that now and read the two pages that we have completed before we describe a new leaf today.

Class rereads the previous day's writing together while Heather points to each word: "I found a big, green, pointy, beautiful leaf. I found a yellow and green leaf that looks like a fan."

Part 2: Initiate Sentence Building

Heather: Today we are going to describe another leaf. [She pins the new leaf on the easel above the sentence strips.] Take out your magnifying glass. [Each student pretends to hold a magnifying glass.] We will write like scientists again, which means we are going to think hard about what we notice and then we will describe the leaf carefully. What can you say about this leaf?

Part 3: Prompt and Negotiate Discussion

The students begin sharing what they notice: It's brown. It's yellow. I see a little green. Heather summarizes and continues to prompt their thinking.

Heather: We have talked about color: brown, yellow, a little green. What other *properties* can we describe?

Student: This is a long leaf.

Student: It looks like an oval.

Heather: Now we are describing its *shape*.

Heather helps them synthesize their ideas.

Heather: I heard yellow, brown, oval shape, long. How can we put these ideas together? Let's start with our pattern: I found a...

Student: I found a oval, long leaf.

Heather: I found *an* oval, long leaf. Can we add color to that?

Student: I found a yellow, oval, long leaf.

Student: It's brown too.

Heather: I found a yellow leaf shaped like an oval. Can we add more?

Student: I found a yellow and brown leaf shaped like an oval.

Heather: OK! Now you are carefully describing color AND shape in one sentence. [She repeats the sentence, emphasizing each word slowly.] I found a yellow and brown leaf shaped like an oval.

Sample Book About Collected Leaves (Kindergarten)

Part 4: Wrap-Up

Heather repeats the final sentence again.

Heather: I like that we put a lot of our ideas together to describe color and shape in one sentence. Can we all say our sentence again?

The class says it together with Heather leading.

Heather: Now shake your hands out and put them up high. Let's say it again and count the words.

The class repeats the sentence and counts the words with their fingers.

Heather: Wow! 10 plus 1. That's 11. We are going to write 11 words. Let's do it!

Next, listen in while Christy and her second graders compose an informational piece about an ancient town they visited on a field trip.

LISTEN IN ON A LESSON: Grade 2

Experience

The second graders took a field trip to Qibao, an ancient town in China. (Note: These students attend an international school in Shanghai.)

Prewrite

Christy explained to students that they would be writing a report about Qibao. They already had written a retelling of the field trip, and she clarified how they were different. The emphasis for this piece was to explain "the most important things" about this town to someone who has never been there.

Compose

Part 1: Transition Into Compose

Christy: We already finished our retelling of the trip. We told what happened when we went there. Now our report will give *information* on Qibao. We need to tell someone who has never been there the most important things. This time we will not need past-tense verbs like we used in our retelling.

Part 2: Initiate Sentence Building

Christy: We need to begin our report with a topic sentence. We want to introduce our paragraph by telling our readers from the beginning what we are writing about. Who can get us started with a topic sentence?

Part 3: Prompt and Negotiate Discussion

Student: I'm giving you information about Qibao.

Christy: Well, you are right. We are giving information to our readers. But when we write a report, we are writing only about the topic, not about ourselves.

Student: Things in Qibao don't cost a lot.

Christy: That is true, but that's not our whole paragraph. We might include this idea in our report, but the topic sentence needs to introduce the main idea we are writing about.

Student:	This is a story about Qibao.
Christy:	That is the general idea. But remember, we are not writing a story. If I were to write a topic sentence for a report about Disney World, I might say: Disney is a theme park in Hong Kong. This topic sentence tells the Where and the What. It tells the topic for our whole report. Then the rest of the paragraph would be details about that big idea. Let's try to do this for Qibao.
Student:	Qibao is a waterfront town in Shanghai, China.
Christy:	Yes! Why is this a thoughtful topic sentence for our report?
Student:	It tells where.
Student:	And what!
Student:	It's also an ancient town.
Christy:	Ancient. That's a helpful word because it is both specific and important.

The class has a brief discussion about the meaning of the word *ancient*.

Christy:	How can we add *ancient* to our topic sentence of "Qibao is a waterfront town in Shanghai, China"?
Student:	Qibao is a waterfront, ancient town in Shanghai, China.

Part 4: Wrap-Up

Christy repeats the final sentence again. The class says it together with Christy leading. The boys say it. The girls say it.

| Christy: | This is a strong sentence to introduce our report. Let's write it, beginning with an indent! |

Share the Pen

The students write the first sentence. (Note: When the sentence is written fully, students move back into Compose again and build the second sentence and write it during this same interactive writing session.)

Informational Report About a Field Trip (Grade 2)

Now, we listen in on Pinnecko working with her fourth graders as they craft a summary based on an informational text read together during their ELA period.

Experience

As part of her district's curriculum, the class had read together excerpts from the text *Toys! Amazing Stories Behind Some Great Inventions* by Don Wulffson during their ELA periods.

The Slinky

There are several events that led to the invention of the slinky. First, Richard James was hired by the U.S. Navy to invent a device that would stabilize ships. When he failed, he used springs to help with the resistance. Then he accidentally knocked the spring off the shelf. *Instead of it falling to the ground like he thought, it walked coil over coil down the shelf.*

Summary of Informational Text (Grade 4)
(Italicized sentence is the focus of the Listen in on a Lesson)

Prewrite

The students planned to write a summary of one of the chapters. The summary would serve as an exemplar for the class as students continued to work on this grade-level writing skill. Pinnecko selected the chapter about the slinky. First, they created a list of the important sequence of events that were described in the chapter. They referred back to the list during Compose. (Note: The Prewrite for this piece was its own 30-minute lesson that occurred the day before Compose began.)

Compose

Part 1: Transition Into Compose

The class rereads the sentences that have been written already. (Note: The first four sentences have been written already.)

Pinnecko: OK, we are ready to pick up from where we left off yesterday. Let's move on to our next sentence. Let's think about what happened when Richard James knocked the spring off the shelf.

Part 2: Initiate Sentence Building

Pinnecko: We need to write a sentence describing that moment. Take a look at the list we made. What happened when he knocked the spring off the shelf? Anyone have some ideas?

Part 3: Prompt and Negotiate Discussion

Student: It fell off the shelf in an interesting way?

Student: It walked down like a slinky?

Pinnecko: Well, OK, yes, it did fall off the shelf in an interesting way. And, yes, it did have the movement of a slinky. But remember, at this point in time, it isn't a slinky yet. Richard James is working with a spring. So we can't say that it falls off the shelf as a slinky. Let's go back to our list. What words did we use to describe the movement the spring had as it fell?

Student: It walked "coil over coil"!

Pinnecko:	Yes, that's it. Very vivid language. I can actually see that motion when I read those words. Coil over coil [Pinnecko moves her arms to demonstrate what she envisions as she reads that phrase.] Let's use that phrase in our sentence. OK, now, did Richard James knock the spring off on purpose or was it an accident?
Class:	An accident!
Pinnecko:	Right, so what did he *think* would happen when it fell?
Student:	He probably thought it would just fall on the ground.
Pinnecko:	Yes, I agree. And, that's what makes this moment so surprising for him. He wasn't expecting it. So how can we combine these two ideas together? How can we say this?
Student:	It didn't fall on the ground. It walked coil over coil?
Student:	He was surprised when it walked coil over coil?
Student:	Instead of falling on the ground, it walked coil over coil?
Student:	I like that one!
Pinnecko:	We're doing some good thinking here. Let's see if we can be a bit more descriptive in terms of Richard James. Let's build off of this: "Instead of it falling on the ground like…"
Student:	Like he thought it would!
Pinnecko:	OK, that works. Let's listen to this beginning: "Instead of it falling on the ground like he thought, it…." What do we say next?
Student:	It walked coil over coil.
Student:	Down the shelf!
Pinnecko:	Yes. Let's put that all together. Listen to what we have: "Instead of it falling on the ground like he thought, it walked coil over coil down the shelf." What do you think?
Student:	That sounds good!!
Student:	I like it!

Part 4: Wrap-Up

Pinnecko repeats the sentence again for the class. She then writes it on a sticky note so that she and her students will remember it exactly for Share the Pen.

Pinnecko:	This is a well-written sentence that captures the moment nicely. The reader will know that Richard James was surprised, and the reader will have a good picture of how the spring moved "coil over coil." I like how we worked together and combined ideas. Let's get this written down.

Challenges of Compose

Although every phase of the lesson offers unique learning opportunities, there are challenges as well. The Compose part of the lesson may sound like a natural conversation, but it takes intentional work to facilitate this well. You want to engage all of your students and support their learning while keeping the pace of the lesson moving along. Finding the right balance between offering too much support and not offering enough support takes practice. Being able to choose the final sentence sometimes requires delicate negotiation. Remember that you do not need students to agree unanimously on the sentence. Rather, you pull the ideas from them, ask them questions, and think aloud to teach them how to compose. Ultimately, however, you are in charge and need to recognize when the sentence works well.

As we explained earlier, skipping this phase entirely by coming into the lesson with the predetermined text written by you would be a missed opportunity. That said, in the interest of pacing or time or because you recognize that the sentence is solid, you will decide when to stop the discussion. At that point, you will pull the students' ideas together and choose the final version of what will be written. Then you explain to your students why the sentence is complete and ready to be written. For example, you might say something like, "OK, I'm hearing several of you say the same ideas, and I think most everyone agrees. We also have some great phrases to include. So here's how we'll put all of these together into one super thoughtful sentence. We'll say...." Finding the balance among collaborating, negotiating, and scaffolding can feel messy, but you and your students *will* get comfortable with this over time.

Planning for Compose

Much of the teaching during Compose is in the moment. You do not know your students' ideas or how they will craft sentences until you are actually writing together. However, although the spontaneity is both exciting and challenging, you can and should still plan ahead. There are several aspects to consider in advance to ensure a productive Compose session. Table 7 addresses these planning points and provides a list of questions to guide you.

Table 7 Planning for Compose

Planning Point	Questions to Guide You
Product Goals	• Will the piece be completed in a single session? (e.g., a single sentence, one paragraph) • Will the piece evolve over multiple sessions? (e.g., multipage book, multiple paragraph piece) • What will the final piece be? (e.g., a class book, a list, an exemplar for a particular genre you are studying, a report, a letter/e-mail to be sent) • How do you plan to use this piece once it's completed? What will you do with it? (e.g., display it, share it with the audience, use it as teaching tool)
Craft Elements	• What elements of craft do you want to be sure to include in the lesson? • What does your curriculum tell you about craft that your writers need to know and practice?
Sentence Length and Complexity	• Approximately how long will your sentence be? • What is an appropriate challenge for sentence length/complexity for your writers?
Thinking Ahead to Share the Pen	• What conventions do you need to address? • How might you craft a sentence that includes those conventions to practice during Share the Pen?
Differentiated Instruction	• Which student(s) will benefit from the craft elements that may arise during Compose? • Which student(s) do you need to engage around oral language? • Which student(s) have a lot to say about the ideas for the piece? • Whom do you want to draw into the conversation? Who might benefit from the "safe practice" structure of Compose?

Product Goals

As you plan for Compose, keep in mind the final written product you envision. If this will be a single-session lesson, then the text to be written must fit all of the goals you are prioritizing and come together efficiently. If this piece of writing will be completed over multiple sessions, consider how you would like Compose to evolve over the course of the writing. There may be different Compose goals each session. Thinking about how you intend to use this piece after it is completed is also important. You may plan to share it with the intended audience, organize it into a class book, or display it as an exemplar in your classroom. Having the end result in mind enables you to create a skeletal plan for Compose.

Craft Elements

The craft of writing takes center stage during Compose. Thus, it follows that you want to be very clear on the craft elements you hope to include. Knowing, for example, that students struggle to use a unique or passionate voice in their writing should guide you to prompt for creative and interesting ways to write your sentence. Or if your students are struggling to organize their ideas well, your Compose session can emphasize how to evaluate multiple ideas and group them in a logical way. For our youngest writers, the craft goals may be learning to put ideas down on paper in a succinct way that stays on topic.

Table 8 Teaching for Craft (Grades PreK–2)

Craft Elements	Possible Teaching Points
Ideas and Organization	• Write about topics that are personally important • Communicate the main points clearly so audience understands • Provide descriptive details to make the writing more interesting or informative • Stay on topic • Present ideas in logical sequence • Write beginning, middle (series of things happening), and end • Write an engaging beginning and satisfying closing • Organize a text in various ways for various purposes (e.g., friendly letter vs. narrative vs. list and procedures) • Use features to guide readers (e.g., title, dedication, author's page) • Use simple words to show passage of time (e.g., *then*, *next*)
Sentence Fluency	• Make sure sentences sound right (i.e., correct grammar) • Write short and long sentences • Begin sentences in different ways
Word Choice	• Vary the writing by choosing alternative words for overused words (e.g., *nice*, *fun*, *cool*, *said*) • Use vocabulary appropriate for the topic • Use words that paint a picture and appeal to our senses • Try out phrases from familiar stories or texts • Use dialogue when appropriate to add to meaning
Voice	• Write like one would speak • Share thoughts and feelings about a topic • State ideas/information in unique and surprising ways • Use underlining and bold print to convey meaning • Write directly to your audience (e.g., Do you like summer?)

As we mentioned earlier, although you will not know the exact words your students will offer during Compose, the craft elements students need to know and practice must be considered ahead of time and applied strategically when the moment arises. Table 8 and Table 9, informed by the work of Pinnell and Fountas (2011) and Spandel (2013), provide a menu of possible teaching points for writers in grades PreK–5. As you can see, there are numerous opportunities for craft instruction.

Sentence Length and Complexity

Before you begin Compose, have a general idea of the length and complexity of the sentence or sentences you intend to write during the day's session. For emergent writers, the length of sentence might range from four to six words. Sentences will then grow and expand as writers develop. Keeping a text "readable" for your students is essential; therefore, you must control the level of text difficulty without oversimplifying it. The optimum sentence

Table 9 Teaching for Craft (Grades 2–5)

Craft Elements	Possible Teaching Points
Ideas and Organization	• Write about topics that are important personally • Incorporate details (supporting information or examples) that are accurate, relevant, and helpful and that enhance meaning • Gather information, then write it in own words • Organize a text in various ways for various purposes (e.g., sequences, categories, how-to, compare and contrast, problem and solution) • Use a variety of leads to hook and engage readers (e.g., direct, engaging, purposeful) • Use a variety of closures to satisfy readers (e.g., surprise or circular) • Use thoughtful titles, headings, and table of contents • Use both simple and complex transitional words for time flow (e.g., *then*, *after*, *because of this*, *the next day*, *finally*)
Sentence Fluency	• Use memorable language: vivid, striking, or unexpected • Show through language instead of telling • Cite ideas or sentences from other writers/texts • Use both simple and complex sentences to enhance the flow of the piece
Word Choice	• Vary the writing by choosing alternative words for overused words (e.g., *happy*, *fun*, *like*, *said*) • Try out words and phrases from familiar authors and texts • Use precise vocabulary appropriate to the topic • Use strong verbs • Include sophisticated words beyond grade-level spelling
Voice	• State ideas/information in unique and surprising ways • Use punctuation (e.g., ellipses, dashes, end marks) to interest and engage readers • Use voice to influence meaning and to provoke strong reader response

may be just beyond what many students could read independently. That said, students will be able to read these pieces because they were involved actively in their creation. The instructional lift provided by the Compose session allows students to advance both their reading *and* writing skills.

Thinking Ahead to Share the Pen

Although Compose focuses on craft, as you plan for this phase you will need to do a bit of forward thinking by considering the conventions you want to include during Share the Pen. You want to craft a sentence that offers your students the opportunity to learn and practice the important conventions they need. During Compose, you work to set up a sentence that will offer these opportunities later in the lesson.

For example, you try to include high-frequency words that your students are learning to spell or words that include spelling principles that you have been practicing. Maybe your class is learning about exclamation points and commas, and this sentence offers an authentic place to practice these concepts. Again, even though you do not know the exact words that will be offered for the sentence, as you skillfully navigate the text to be written with students, you keep the convention opportunities on your radar too.

Differentiated Instruction

A final point to consider when planning for Compose is, of course, your students. Knowing which students to engage during a lesson is essential. Plan for this ahead of time by reading your students' independent writing frequently. Take notice of the students who need support in any of the craft areas you are prioritizing in the day's lesson. Be sure to seize the opportunities to engage students who have much to say aloud but may struggle with writing down their words. Plan for a range of talk opportunities (e.g., "turn and talks" or partners) so that quiet and reserved students have authentic ways to participate. If you know the five or six students who must participate, jot their names down to cue your memory in the moment. This important planning allows you to differentiate your instruction and maximize the lesson for all students.

Final Thoughts

Compose is the time for you and your students to work together to negotiate the precise language of the sentence to be written. You focus on the craft of writing as you support and advance students' ideas, organization, sentence fluency, word choice, and voice. This part of the lesson may sound like a natural conversation, but it takes technique and advanced planning to facilitate well. Finding the balance among collaborating, negotiating, and scaffolding can feel messy, but you and your students will get comfortable with this over time.

As students develop further in their writing, the teaching within Compose mirrors this growth. The sentences crafted will be longer and will include multiple ideas, more complex language, and interesting stylistic choices. Compose is well worth your time and energy, as it provides an extraordinary opportunity to practice the writing process by considering the essential elements of craft using a piece that holds both meaning and relevance. Allow yourself to enjoy this collaborative experience while making the most of the teaching opportunities.

CHAPTER 6

Share the Pen

A finished piece of writing holds power if, and only if, the intended audience can decipher its meaning. Conventions matter! Share the Pen is the place in the lesson where we attend to this essential part of the writing. As you work through this step, consider these questions: How do we teach and practice important writing conventions? What language and teaching moves support this phase of the lesson? In what ways do we plan and prepare for Share the Pen?

When the precise language for the sentence has been finalized, the interactive writing lesson moves into Share the Pen. During this step, the text is written with a technique unique to interactive writing in which the teacher and students take turns with the pen or marker. With older and more fluent writers, Share the Pen can be modified to become Share the Keyboard, where the teacher and students type using a keyboard or touchscreen with text displayed on a screen or interactive whiteboard. In all cases, the teacher writes or types some of the text and then chooses students to write or type at points of high instructional value.

The teaching and learning that occur during Share the Pen focus on the conventions of writing. Although the teaching emphasis differs from Compose, they are similar in that the planning done ahead of time and in the moment is strategic. Share the Pen is informed by what you know about your students, your curriculum expectations, and the characteristics of good writing.

WHAT TEACHERS ARE SAYING

I know when I do interactive writing, I am guaranteed to teach spelling, handwriting, concepts about print, punctuation, and other writing conventions in 10 minutes. It is such powerful teaching for my emergent readers and writers.   —Amy (Kindergarten)

Share the Pen: A Time for Teaching Conventions

During Share the Pen, the text is written down using an innovative technique where you and your students take turns *sharing* the pen, marker, or keyboard. You write parts of the message and then select individual students to write at points of high instructional value. Simultaneously, you lead a strategic discussion with all of your students around conventions. This discussion is informed by two key areas: (1) what your students must know and understand about conventions and (2) by the convention opportunities that exist in the sentence to be written. Let's begin by considering the conventions that all writers need and then explore how Share the Pen supports this.

The Conventions of Writing

As teachers, we all have read a piece of writing that holds strong ideas, includes exceptional words or phrases, or is filled with passion, but we struggle to find the message because spelling errors pervade the piece. Or we are at a loss to make meaning from what is on the page because punctuation is left out, letters are haphazardly formed, or the words are crowded together without clear spaces or margins. Many of us may even feel the urge to pull out our "red pens" and quickly fix the errors for the writer. There is clarity around what is correct and incorrect; convention errors can feel glaringly obvious. The rule-oriented world of writing conventions is far different territory from the often subjective world of writing craft.

When we think about conventions, we include the range of important skills that will either advance or hinder the final product. Spelling, grammar, capitalization, punctuation, handwriting, word processing, and text layout all fall under the umbrella of conventions. All writers in grades PreK–5 need to work on conventions, although the ones they are learning become progressively more complex and sophisticated. Spending time on the teaching of conventions has a positive impact on the overall quality of the writing (Graham & Harris, 2013; Graham & Perin, 2007a; Saddler, 2013; Schlagal, 2013). Tables 10 and 11 are informed by the work of Pinnell and Fountas (2011) and Spandel (2013). They provide an abundant list of important conventions that interactive writing supports.

Teaching for Conventions During Share the Pen

During Share the Pen, you and your students share the responsibility of writing the sentence. Because you know the exact text to be written and you know the needs of your student writers, you are intentional about which parts of the sentence you will write and which parts will be written by a student. You also are intentional about which particular student will write. The dynamic teaching done in this phase of the lesson is both individualized and aligned with grade-level expectations. You teach the whole class the required grade-level conventions while providing important and timely scaffolds for the individual student selected to write.

Table 10 Conventions to Teach During Share the Pen (Grades PreK–2)

Conventions	Possible Teaching Points for Grades K–2
Spelling	• Spell grade-appropriate high-frequency words correctly • Say and hear sounds in words • Spell patterns (e.g., common word endings, vowel combinations, blends and digraphs) • Teach strategies for spelling (e.g., using known words for analogy, clapping syllables, visualizing words to makes sure they look right)
Grammar	• Write a complete sentence with noun and verb • Consider prepositional phrases (e.g., to the store) • Select the appropriate tense (past, present, or future)
Capitalization	• Use capital letters for first word of sentence, days of week, months, cities, states, names of people and specific places, titles, headings, first word of greeting in a letter, etc.
Punctuation	• Consider how punctuation helps a reader understand text • Use periods, exclamation points, and question marks as ending marks • Use quotation marks appropriately • Use apostrophes in contractions and possessives
Handwriting	• Form upper- and lowercase letters efficiently • Hold pen or marker with correct grip
Text Layout	• Put appropriate space between words • Write words left to right, top to bottom

Table 11 Conventions to Teach During Share the Pen (Grades 2–5)

Conventions	Possible Teaching Points for Grades 2–5
Spelling	• Spell grade-appropriate high-frequency words correctly, consulting references as needed • Use correct spelling for possessives, contractions, compound words, studied words (spelling lists), or relevant vocabulary
Grammar	• Use a range of complete sentences (simple, compound, and complex) • Incorporate grade-level grammar rules for subject/verb agreement and noun/pronoun agreement, and the correct use of prepositional phrases, adjectives, adverbs, and plurals (simple and complex) • Select the appropriate tense (past, present, or future)
Capitalization	• Use capital letters for first word of sentence, days of week, months, cities, states, names of people and specific places, titles, headings, first word of greeting in a letter, etc.
Punctuation	• Consider how punctuation helps a reader understand text • Use periods, exclamation points, and question marks as ending marks • Use quotation marks appropriately • Use commas to identify a series or to introduce clauses • Use ellipses to show pause or anticipation • Use dashes and ellipses for emphasis or to slow down the text for readers • Use periods after abbreviations • Use apostrophes in contractions and possessives
Handwriting and Word Processing	• Form upper- and lowercase letters efficiently • Begin and develop efficient keyboarding skills • Use technology to plan, draft, revise, edit, and publish
Text Layout	• Arrange print (and illustrations) to support meaning • Use underlines, boldfaced, or italicized print or capital letters to help readers notice important information, titles, headings, and subheadings • Consider the optimum choices for layout, spacing, and size of print

Teacher Shares the Pen With Student (Grade 3)

Teacher Models How to Write "We" While Student Shares the Pen (PreK)

Student Leading the Class in Rereading (PreK)

At particular points chosen by you, a student takes the pen, marker, or keyboard and transcribes whatever amount of the text that you believe will be "just right" in terms of an appropriate instructional challenge. Early in the year, you give all of your students the opportunity to be the one to write or type. This helps build confidence and solidifies the routine of interactive writing. Very soon after, however, the selection of students is informed by data. You always support the selected student by watching closely and encouraging him or her to think before writing. Sometimes, you might model on a small whiteboard what to write. Every student completes the writing feeling successful.

Simultaneously, you engage the whole class in Share the Pen by highlighting and emphasizing the writing conventions being practiced as the sentence is being written. You move back and forth between the individual writer and the whole class intentionally. For example, you might ask the class to watch closely as the student writes, while at other times you use a small whiteboard to teach the convention to the class while the student is writing. You can also have students do a quick turn-and-talk about a particular convention while you quickly support the student if he or she is stuck or uncertain. For older students, individual whiteboards work well for them to practice the skill or technique while the student writes an entire phrase or segment of the sentence.

During Share the Pen, rereading of the sentence is done multiple times to practice fluency and deepen comprehension. This rereading helps writers keep in mind the whole meaning of their message while they are working on the details of inscribing. The cycle of selecting a student to share the pen or keyboard continues until the sentence is complete.

Share the Pen: A Powerful Next Step!

Share the Pen is an innovative approach to guided writing that provides the critical supportive step between modeling writing for your students and sending them off to write independently. This step in the lesson is powerful because the students have the opportunity to focus on conventions in an intensive but authentic setting as well as develop their overall language and literacy skills, including reading and oral language. They also continue to work on the writing process. Share the Pen facilitates three powerful instructional actions. First, it pulls together discrete parts of your literacy curriculum within an authentic context. Second, it magnifies what it means to edit. Third, it uses an innovative approach to guided practice in writing.

Pull Together Discrete Parts of Your Literacy Curriculum Within an Authentic Context

Interactive writing links all aspects of your literacy curriculum together. Because pieces written during interactive writing are meant to be reread by students and are intended for a broader audience, standard spelling and punctuation are important. Therefore, a wide range of conventions are explicitly highlighted and taught during this phase. Share the Pen addresses these as they occur. While transcribing the message, students work on *all* convention elements (e.g., spelling, punctuation, handwriting) at once. As you choose your teaching points during this part of a lesson, it is a perfect time for you to tie together lessons from all aspects of your literacy curriculum.

Foundational literacy skills such as phonemic awareness and phonics hold a paramount role for developing writers (Cunningham, 2011). These can be integrated seamlessly into Share the Pen. For example, as emergent writers work to sound out letters and words, you remind them of the work you have done around specific phonemes. You also support their phonics and handwriting development by reminding them of how to record their sounds into letters. As more fluent writers take on multisyllabic words, you pull any relevant skills from their word work or spelling curriculum to support them. The same logic holds for grammar and punctuation work: If you have been working on these issues in other parts of your literacy teaching and they subsequently surface during the interactive writing lesson, be sure to highlight these connections for your students!

Although isolated teaching of conventions has merits, relying exclusively on this approach is problematic (Brozo, 2003). Share the Pen, however, takes place within an authentic context of *real* writing attached to *real* purpose. Students practice and apply conventions anchored to a writing piece that holds meaning for them while synthesizing what they are learning in many other literacy-based lessons throughout their day. This method engages students to learn and use conventions in order to improve their writing (Bromley, 2011).

In a similar fashion, students connect reading and writing as they read through the piece multiple times. They initially work on decoding and then move into fluency work as they reread. Comprehension is also highlighted, as rereading reminds students of the sentence and prompts them to recall what word or phrase comes next. Meaning is always central in the writers' minds. When you step back, you see that Share the Pen is instructionally rich. Multiple literacy skills and strategies are applied and practiced while working through this phase of the lesson.

Magnify What It Means to Edit

As described in Chapter 5, the opportunity to slow down and unpack a step within the writing process is a key part of interactive writing. During Share the Pen, you magnify how to edit your writing. The in-the-moment editing techniques, such as rereading each word or sentence and checking spelling carefully, allow your students to practice what real writers do—fix mistakes in real time. We cannot emphasize this point enough: the convention errors that occur during this phase are teachable moments!

Use an Innovative Approach to Guided Practice in Writing

Finally, as described in Chapter 2, interactive writing is a guided teaching practice. This unique guidance stands out most strikingly within the Share the Pen phase when you teach conventions by sharing the pen or keyboard with your students. Other teaching methods in writing, such as language experience approach, modeled writing, and shared writing, offer important learning opportunities for students. Each of these practices has deeply informed the development and evolution of interactive writing (McCarrier et al., 2000). That said, we cannot understate the power of guided experiences for developing writers (Reutzel, 2011). If we agree that working within a child's zone of proximal development will propel him or her forward, then interactive writing is an *essential* teaching practice to have in our "teaching toolbox."

Teaching Moves Within Share the Pen

Although Share the Pen follows a predictable pattern and flow, it does not follow a tight linear sequence. A collection of teaching moves informs how you work through this part of the lesson. You decide which conventions to teach, select the student who will write, engage the class, and write parts of the sentence yourself. Throughout this phase, you reread what is written, correct mistakes at the point of error, and connect all of it back to students' independent writing.

Decide Which Conventions to Teach

Once you know the specific message that will be written, you quickly determine the conventions that you will have your students write. Remember, an effective Share the Pen does not mean having the students write every letter of every word or attending to every convention issue that arises. Instead, it is characterized by a close match between teaching and your students' needs and your curriculum. Because you want to make the most of the time your students are engaged in this activity, do not spend time on conventions they already know or conventions far beyond their basic understanding. Your goal is to choose clear examples to highlight particular principles about conventions.

Select the Student for Share the Pen/Share the Keyboard

You thoughtfully choose the student who will write or type. It is essential that the scribing holds a specific value for a student's individual writing development. For example, an emergent writer might contribute single letters, letter clusters, whole words, or punctuation, whereas a more fluent writer is often capable of adding longer phrases or the entire sentence.

> ## WHAT TEACHERS ARE SAYING
>
> Everyone is involved. Even if they can't write the entire sentence, they can at least contribute something small. —Sonja (Grade 4)

In the primary grades, choosing a student can be informed by connecting his or her name with a principle that is being taught. (Table 12 explains more about why and how to do this.) For example, when needing to add -*er* to a word, selecting a student who has those letters in his or her name (e.g., Oliv*er* or Christoph*er*) is an optimal choice. Or choose the student who has been working on punctuation in his or her independent writing to scribe the period or question mark in the piece being written. The rule of the thumb is to select the student who will benefit most from practicing the convention that needs to be written at that moment.

Engage All Students Around Conventions

As we have described, in this step of the lesson, one student is selected at a time to write a portion of the text. This means that the rest of the students will

Table 12 Name Chart: A Powerful Resource During Share the Pen (Grades PreK–2)

The What	• A name chart is a chart listing the names of students in the class.
	• How to make a name chart:
	  ○ Write names on chart paper in alphabetical order.
	  ○ Print clearly so the chart is a model for writing letters.
	  ○ Put first letter in contrasting color to highlight the beginning of a word and capital letters.
	  ○ Option: Put names on cards organized alphabetically in a pocket chart
	  ○ Begin by using first names. (May include last names in late grade 1 or grade 2.)

The Why	• Most important word for a child when first learning language
	• Helps with word study: Link well-known names with unfamiliar words when reading and writing
	• Helps with basic understanding about written language.
	For example:
	  ○ My name is a word
	  ○ A word is written the same way each time
	  ○ A word is made up of a sequence of letters
	  ○ Not all words have the same number of letters
	  ○ Letters and sounds are connected
	  ○ One word can help you read and write other words

The How	• Study the names in your class and brainstorm all of the principles you can teach on the basis of your class list. They will range from simple concepts like letter knowledge (e.g., letter names, sounds, formation) to more complex (e.g., vowel combinations). Be ready to use these ideas when the opportunity arises.
	• Use your students' names to build on what they know about words and letters. They can use the "known" to figure out the "unknown."
	• Use the name chart to teach progressively more complex concepts as writers advance.
	• Following is a small sampling of principles aligned with the name chart shown in this table:
	  ○ Think of Benjamin or Annabel if you want to write the letter *B/b*
	  ○ Words that sound alike are often spelled alike (*Jack* and *Zack*)
	  ○ Shayla helps you spell *sheep*
	  ○ *Ph* sounds like /f/ as in *Sophia*
	  ○ Andrew and Alexandria help you spell *and*
	  ○ Think of Lindy or Lily for *y* that sounds like /e/ at the end of a word
	  ○ *oo* is like Oona

Room 6 Kids

Alexandria
Andrew
Annabel
Benjamin
Christopher
Collins
Daria
Diego
Flynn
Hans
Jack
Lindy
Lily
Maxwell
Oliver
Oona
Quinn
Roan
Samyukt
Shayla
Sophia
Trevor
Tripp
Yesslee
Zack

Note. Adapted from the work of Bloodgood (1999), Clay (1975), Coker (2013), McCarrier et al. (2000), and Pinnell and Fountas (1998).

need to be engaged so that the lesson continues to be focused and efficient. There are multiple ways to keep your students engaged thoughtfully during these moments. For example, you might highlight high-frequency words by telling your students that these are "snap" words—words they should know and be able to spell in a snap. You might demonstrate how to clap out the individual sounds in a word in order to determine its spelling. Table 13 provides a detailed list of how to engage all students during Share the Pen. In every lesson, you will use a range of engagement strategies. As you use interactive writing in your classroom, you will discover what works best with your students.

The overriding theme in these strategies is that students are thinking about the text that is being written. They may visualize the word or phrase, whisper it to a partner, or write in the air or on individual marker boards. Each of these experiences can deepen students' understanding of writing conventions while connecting them again with the overall message of the piece. Just be mindful not to move on to a new point while one student is still writing. Stick with the convention being addressed at the moment.

Table 13 Engagement Strategies That Support Writing Conventions

Kinesthetic Teaching	• "Write" in the air or on the floor/rug; (spelling) • Clap each syllable in a word
Making Connections About Words	• Connect to other words with similar spelling patterns or principles (e.g., rhyming words, words that have similar beginning sounds, homonyms) • Analyze the word itself (e.g., count number of letters, identify beginning/ending letter, identify the root word, notice any suffixes and prefixes) • Make connections to a name chart
Practice Strategies That Writers Use	• Tap out multisyllabic words • Say a word slowly to listen for its sounds • Visualize how a word looks (spelling) • Spell high-frequency ("snap") words quickly (e.g., whip around the class and have individual students spell the word quickly, spell the word aloud together)
Quick Discussion and Elaboration About the Convention Being Written	• Define and clarify the convention itself as it is being written (e.g., capitalization rules, different punctuation options, letter formation) • Elaborate on when and how we might use this convention in other writing (e.g., ask how commas are used in different ways, brainstorm other times when it is important to use a capital letter) • Discuss a range of keyboarding or technology features (e.g., difference between caps lock and shift key, grammar/spelling errors with blue or red underline, using tab, backspace, cursors, space bar)

Write Parts of the Sentence Yourself

Take the pen and write part of the message when that makes sense for instructional goals or the pacing of the lesson. You might choose to think-aloud the parts you write (e.g., "I am going to put in the silent -*e* at the end of this word.") or just keep moving the lesson along by writing quickly and calling up the next student to write the next part of the message that includes a convention you want to highlight.

Reread What Is Written

As a student finishes scribing his or her section of the piece, you quickly select the next student to continue the writing or write a part of the message yourself. Note that an important in-between step occurs before the next student writes. Guided by the student who just scribed, the entire class rereads the word or phrase that has been written thus far. This focus on rereading brings fluency into the lesson in a natural way. It also emphasizes how fluency relates to comprehension (Kuhn & Rasinski, 2011). It prompts students to remember what sound, word, or phrase comes next in their piece.

Correct Mistakes at the Moment of Error

Convention mistakes are a central and natural part of Share the Pen. In all cases, editing of conventions is done at the point of error. If you are using markers and chart paper, have white correcting tape within reach. When a writing error occurs, simply place the tape over the precise location. If you are using an interactive whiteboard, students can "erase" or "tap away" their errors.

When a keyboard is used, this fluid editing work is quite user-friendly. Misspelled words or errors around grammar, punctuation, and spelling often cause a red underline to appear. This alerts the writer that something may be incorrect.

Teacher Writes Part of the Text (Grade 3)

Using White Correcting Tape for Real-Time Editing (Grade 3)

Students can use the keyboard tools to correct mistakes, resulting in a seamless editing experience.

Connect to Students' Independent Writing

A critical piece of Share the Pen is linking the instruction back to your students' independent writing. To do this, remind students to practice these same convention skills or rules in their writing. This explicitness helps with the transfer of skills from a group setting to the independent work for writers of all ages.

For example, making spaces between words is typically a concept that is emphasized for our youngest writers in PreK–1. In these grades, a student might be selected to be "The Spacer" between every word or every child might have to "put two fingers in the air" before a new word is written to indicate that a space is needed. If this is the case and spaces are emphasized during Share the Pen, you should be sure to say, "See how we are being so careful to put a space between each of our words to make it easy for our readers to understand our message. You need to make a space between each of your words when you write by yourself." This idea holds for upper-grade writers too. For example, if you are working on how to use commas in a series, tell students to do the same when they write on their own.

As you can see, there are numerous teaching moves within Share the Pen, and they require you to juggle many things. Each move holds its own unique and important purpose. The moves will become more automatic as you practice them again and again with your students, and you will feel more comfortable with them over time. This energetic and fast-paced phase of the lesson is packed with learning opportunities.

WHAT TEACHERS ARE SAYING

Interactive writing is a part of my teaching where technology really moves the lesson along. The typing is especially important for my students. I want them to be ready for middle school, where more of what they do will require strong keyboarding skills. I want to put as many tools as I can into their toolboxes.   —Melissa (Grade 5)

How Share the Pen Changes Over Time

As writers grow and develop, it follows that their needs do the same. Although the essential teaching moves within Share the Pen are consistent through the grades, there are three key shifts to consider as writers mature.

Lesson Flow Becomes More Fluid and Dynamic

As noted in Chapter 5, in the primary grades, the interactive writing lesson format is linear. Although you may spend several days working to complete an entire piece, you will typically write one or two simple sentences each time. Because of the age and skill of the students, the writing is done slowly and your students benefit most from simple texts. You agree on a sentence during

Compose and then write it while sharing the pen. You edit the sentence while sharing the pen and then move into Review.

As your students become more fluent writers, there is more flow between Compose and Share the Pen. Depending on your goals, time frame, and the skill of the writers, you might write several sentences or whole paragraphs in one interactive writing lesson. To do this, you move back and forth between Compose and Share the Pen. You negotiate the precise message sentence by sentence and then share the pen or keyboard after each sentence is decided. You continue this cycle until you have completed the lesson for the day.

Pace of Writing Increases

In PreK–1, you and your students share the pen and write the message on a word-by-word or even a letter-by-letter basis. You talk about each word as you go and reread the message after you finish each word. This helps students remember the next word to be written and to check that their writing continues to "make sense." As writers become more fluent, the pace with which they write becomes quicker. By grade 2, one student might come up and write several words or an entire phrase. Alternatively, as mentioned earlier in this chapter, you can write a significant part of the piece if the pacing of the lesson requires.

Technology Is Incorporated

At around grade 3, students often have developed their fine motor skills well enough to write smaller than when they were in the primary grades. This physical development is recognized and integrated as Share the Pen evolves for older writers. Having students write on large chart paper may not make sense. In fact, it may cause confusion or frustration for them to write letters using big print when they most likely have solidified what it means to print or write in cursive in a more conventional size.

Using a Document Camera, Teacher Guides Student (Grade 4)

That said, these writers may still need support on letter formation and spacing. A terrific tool for this is a document camera (e.g. ELMO projector, docucam). With your guidance, students can practice all the important conventions using handwriting appropriate for their development while the text is projected for their classmates to see. This technology is also helpful if you, your school, or your district requires a particular type of lined paper for students to use.

Simply include the optimal paper that you need students to use when they write independently.

As literacy and technology continue to merge and evolve, the opportunity to write using keyboard or touchscreen technology can support faster scribing, efficient revision, and unique presentation options. Students show improvement in their writing over time when they use word processing to write at school (Bangert-Drowns, 1993; Goldberg, Russell, & Cook, 2003; Morphy & Graham, 2012). Thus, an important modification within Share the Pen is the incorporation of typing or keyboarding. Word-processing skills become a meaningful part of teaching during Share the Keyboard. Although technology is not required for upper grades, it can be effective and engaging.

Student Shares the Keyboard (Grade 3)

Listening in on lessons will help illustrate the nuances and emphases in the Share the Pen phase and how these discussions and teaching points change and develop as writers mature. In the first Listen in on a Lesson, Jeff works with his prekindergartners to write a sentence describing an oval.

LISTEN IN ON A LESSON: Prekindergarten

Experience

The students in PreK were studying shapes.

Prewrite

The students planned to make posters to hang around the room. Each poster would describe a different shape.

Compose

For each shape, the class wrote two or three sentences. The students composed one sentence a day.

Share the Pen

The sentence to be written is "It is a squished circle."

NOTICE: For the first word (*it*), Jeff talks about where to start writing, letter formation, saying words slowly, capital letters at the beginning of a sentence, space between words, using an

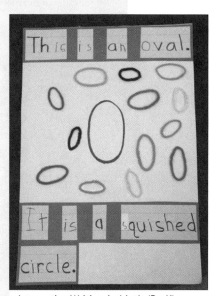

Interactive Writing in Math (PreK)

alphabet linking chart and name chart to help with letter sounds and formation, letter names and letter sounds, and rereading after each word to remember the message. He models key points and then expects students to try them (e.g., saying words slowly).

Jeff: What is the first word we are writing today?

Students: It!

Jeff: That is a word we write all the time. Let's say it slowly and listen to the first sound. First, listen to me say it. [Says *it* slowly to exaggerate two sounds] Now, let's say it together.

Students
and Jeff: It!

Jeff: Listen to me focus on the first sound: I-I-I-It. Now you say the word slowly and listen to first sounds.

Jeff cups his ear to indicate he is listening to the students practice saying the word slowly.

Students: I-i-i.

Jeff: What letter makes the /i/ sound?

Students: I.

Jeff: OK, let's have Andrew come up and write the *I*. What kind of *I* will he need?

Student: Big one.

Jeff: We do need a capital *I*. Why do we need to write an uppercase *I* here?

Student: Because it's the first letter in our sentence.

Jeff: We always begin with a capital letter and then most of our other letters will be lowercase. Let's make the big *I*. Andrew, where will you write that letter? [Andrew points to the far left of the top sentence strip.] Andrew knew that we always begin to write over here. [Points to starting place] I'm going to write an uppercase *I* on the whiteboard. Put your fingers up, and let's write it in the air. [All students put a finger up. Andrew writes on sentence strip.] *I* is a tall letter, so let's start at the top and pull down, across, across.

Students write in the air while saying "pull down, across, across."

Jeff: Let's say the word *it* again and really listen for the last sound. Listen to me say it slowly, and then you can say it.

Jeff says *it* slowly, emphasizing the *t*. Then he cups his ear and the students say the word slowly.

Jeff:	What is that sound at the end of the word?
Students:	T-t-t.
Jeff:	What letter makes the /t/ sound?
Students:	T.
Jeff:	Yes, it sounds like t-t-t-turtle. [Points to alphabet linking chart] Stacy, can you come up and make the *t*? Stacy has a *t* in her name. [Points to "Stacy" on chart] Is *t* a tall letter or a short letter?
Students:	Tall!
Jeff:	Let's put our fingers way up to make that tall *t*. Then pull down and across.

Students write *t* in the air. Jeff writes it on the whiteboard. Stacy writes it on the sentence strip. They all repeat "pull down and across."

Jeff:	We finished our first word. Let's read it!

Stacy takes the pointer and points to the word *it*, and the class reads.

Jeff:	Let's say our sentence again and think about the next word.
Students:	"It *IS*."
Jeff:	What do we need before our next word?
Students:	A space!
Jeff:	We *always* need to remember putting a space between our words. Marcus, can you come up and be our spacer? We will get ready to write our next word, *is*.

NOTICE: For the second word (*is*), Jeff talks about spelling a high-frequency word, using the word wall as a resource, adding spaces between words, and rereading after each word to remember the message.

Jeff Calls Up a Student to Be a Spacer

Jeff:	The word *is*. We have written that word so many times this week. We even put it on our word wall yesterday! How do we write the word *is*?
Student:	I-s.
Jeff:	Two letters make the word *is*. Sarah, can you come up and write the word *is*? Will she use uppercase or lowercase letters?
Students:	Lowercase!

Jeff: That's right. Put the uppercase only at the beginning. *Is* is now a snap word for us. You all know this word in a snap.

Jeff writes *is* on the whiteboard. Sarah writes *is* on the paper while looking at the whiteboard for help. Marcus holds two fingers between *It* and *is* to mark the space.

Jeff: While Sarah writes *is*, let's practice writing that snap word. [He quickly calls on three kids to spell *is*.] Again "*i-s, is,*" and if you need to write that word, remember to look at our word wall.

Jeff: Thank you, Marcus, for helping us put in a space between our words. You can sit down. Sarah, you lead us in rereading our message so we can check our work and think about our next word.

Sarah takes the pointer and points to the words *It is* while the class reads.

Jeff: Let's say our sentence again and think about the next word.

Students: "It is *A*."

Jeff: What do we need before our next word?

Students: A space!

Jeff: We need a space again. Terrence will be the spacer this time. And then we write the word *a*. A super, super easy word!

NOTICE: For the third word (*a*), Jeff talks about spelling a high-frequency word, using lowercase letters in the middle of a sentence, using the name chart as a resource, forming letters, adding spaces between words, and rereading to remember the message.

Jeff: *A* is a letter and a word! Do we need a big *a* or a small *a*?

Students: Small.

Jeff: We *do* need a lowercase *a*. Just like in Marina's name. [Points to name on chart] Marina, you come up and make your little *a*. We all will write it on the floor. First, watch me. [Jeff writes *a* on the whiteboard.] Start at the dotted line and pull back, around, up, and down. Now I will watch you.

Marina writes on the paper. Students write on the floor.

Jeff: Thank you for helping us make a space, Terrence. Marina, you lead us in reading our sentence so we can check our writing and remember our next word.

Marina takes the pointer and points to the words. The class rereads and says the next word: "It is a SQUISHED!"

NOTICE: For the fourth word (*squished*), Jeff talks about putting a space between words, saying words slowly and listening for the first sound, connecting to the alphabet chart and name chart, using upper- and lowercase letters, forming letters, and rereading to remember the message.

Jeff:	What do we need before our next word?
Students:	A space!
Jeff:	Yes, we need a space again. Daquan will be the spacer this time. And then we write the word *squished*. This is a tricky word. Let's say this word slowly and listen for the first sound. Listen to me: s-s-s-squished. Now you say it.
Students:	S-S-S-Squished.
Jeff:	What is that letter we hear at the beginning of the word *squished*?
Students:	S.
Jeff:	It's just like the *s* in *sun*. [Points to alphabet linking chart] Savannah, can you come up and write the *s*? But Savannah, your name begins with an uppercase *S*, and we need a lowercase *s* because it is in the middle of our sentence. The big and little *s* look the same, but the little *s* is shorter.

Daquan holds the space. Savannah writes the *s*. Jeff writes the *s* on his whiteboard. He says, "Pull back, in, around, and back around." Savannah makes her *s* backward.

| Jeff: | Oops, you made it lowercase, but it is backward. Let's try again. |

He covers the mistake with white tape, and Savannah writes it again.

| Jeff: | While Savannah writes a lowercase *s* again, let's all write an *s* in the air. Put your fingers on that dotted line in the middle! |

Students write *s* starting on the imaginary dotted line in the air.

| Jeff: | I am going to finish the word *squished*. [He writes the rest of the word quickly.] Savannah, you can lead us in rereading our message. |

Savannah takes the pointer and points to the words. The class rereads and says the next word: "It is a squished CIRCLE!"

NOTICE: For the last word (*circle*), Jeff talks about both directionality and starting a second line on the far left, using a *c* for the /s/ sound, placing a period at the end of the sentence, and rereading to remember message.

Jeff:	*Circle*! A new word! But we ran out of space on our line, so we need to write on the next line, starting over here. [He points to the far left of line two.]
Jeff:	When I say the word c-c-c-circle, it sounds like it starts with an *s*, but it is actually the letter *c*. It's a tricky one. I am going to quickly write *circle*. [Jeff writes.] Now, let's reread our message. Tarik, you come up and lead the class in rereading. [The class reads while Tarik points to each word.] I think we are done! But how will our readers know that? How will they know to stop reading? What do we need?
Student:	A dot.

Jeff:	We need to put a period at the end of our sentence. You should always do that when you are writing. Felix, you come up and make that dot. Where should he put it? Up high? In the middle? On the line?
Students:	On the line!
Jeff:	You all put that dot in the air while Felix writes it on the paper.

NOTICE: To complete Share the Pen, the students work on reading fluency and concepts about print, including concept of a word and directionality. Before students move on to Review, they do several things:

1. Reread the message several times while Jeff points to each word. The whole class reads together. They read it in "a deep voice like a giant" and then in a "whisper voice."

2. Count how many words they wrote.

In the second Listen in on a Lesson, Laurie and her first graders write a sentence in their book about their neighborhood.

LISTEN IN ON A LESSON: Grade 1

Experience

The students took a walking tour of their neighborhood as part of a social studies unit on community.

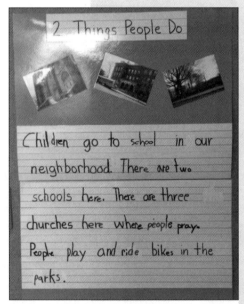

Interactive Writing in Social Studies (Grade 1)

Prewrite

Laurie told her students they would write an informational book to share their discoveries with the school community. The book would be organized by topic (e.g., Homes, Things People Do, Stores and Businesses) and include an index.

Compose

The students wrote one or two sentences a day.

Share the Pen

Sentence to be written is "Children go to school in our neighborhood."

NOTICE: For the first word (*Children*), Laurie talks about connecting sounds to the name chart, saying words slowly to record a letter for each sound, using an uppercase letter at the beginning of a sentence, rereading to check writing, and focusing on meaning.

Laurie:	Listen to *children*. It starts just like Charles's name. CHildren. CHarles. You say that and listen to that /ch/ sound. [The class says "Children, Charles."]

	Charles, you can come up and write the /ch/ sound. What two letters will that be?
Students:	*C-h*.
Laurie:	Should *C* be upper- or lowercase?
Students:	Uppercase.
Laurie:	It is a capital *C* for *Charles* because it's his name, and it is a capital *C* for *Children* because it is the first word in our sentence. While Charles writes *ch*, can you think of any other *C-H* words?

Students say *church* and *cheese*.

| Laurie: | Now let's say this word slowly and listen for the other sounds in the word. |

Laurie guides the students in saying the word slowly over and over to hear the sounds for *i*, *l*, *d*, *r*, and *n*. Laurie tells them there is an *e* before the final *n*. Charles records the rest of the word on the paper while Laurie writes it on a small whiteboard for all to see. When the word is written, Charles uses the pointer to lead the class in rereading what they have written and anticipates the next two words that need to be written.

NOTICE: For the words *go* and *to*, Laurie writes them quickly because they are high-frequency words that the students already know well. She calls on a few students to practice spelling these words and reminds her class that the words are on the wall. They read for meaning and to check work.

| Laurie: | *Go* and *to*—two super-easy snap words for us. I will write these quickly. [While she writes, she calls on two students to spell *go* and two students to spell *to*.] These are words you need to spell correctly in your own writing because they are easy for us, and you can check the word wall. Now let's reread what we have written so far to make sure we have not made any mistakes and think about what to write next. |

Laurie points as the students read "Children go to SCHOOL."

NOTICE: For the word *school*, Laurie talks about consonant blend of *sc*, saying words slowly to listen to sounds, the vowel combination of *oo*, and rereading to check work and to remember meaning.

Laurie:	Let me hear you say that word slowly and listen for the two sounds you hear at the beginning. [Students say "Sc, Sc."] What two letters make that sound?
Student:	*S-k*.
Laurie:	Sounds like *s-k*. It could be, but this time it is *s-c*. Ayisha, you can come up and write the *s-c*. [Ayisha writes as Laurie writes *sc* on the small board.] You also put an *h* after the *c*. It's a silent letter in the word *school*. Now let's say the word again and listen for the sound in the middle of the word. [Laurie and the students say "Scho-o-o-ol."] What two letters make the /oo/ sound?

Student:	*O-w.*
Laurie:	That's *ow* like *how* or *now*. We need the /oo/ sound like *moon*.
Student:	*O-o.*
Laurie:	It is two *O*s together that make the /oo/ sound. [Calls up student to write *oo*] *OO* is in *moon*. Can you think of any other words with *oo* like *school* and *moon*? [Students think of *soon* and *spoon*.] *School* is a word that we keep saying over and over to listen for every sound. Say it again and listen for the last sound in the word. [Students say "School-l-l-l." The same student who wrote *oo* finishes the word while Laurie writes it on the small board.]
Laurie:	You did a really good job saying that word over and over and writing at least one letter for every sound you hear. That is exactly what you need to do when you are writing by yourself.

Then, that student leads the class in rereading what has been written so far and adding the next word: "Children go to school IN." Laurie quickly writes the high-frequency word *in* and has the students practice spelling it.

Laurie:	*In* is another snap word.

She calls on three kids to spell *in* quickly as she writes it on the sentence strip. Then she leads the class in rereading.

NOTICE: For the word *our*, Laurie teaches the /ow/ sound, listening to the end sound of a word, saying words slowly, using the word on the word wall as an indication that it is a word students need to know, adding spaces between words, and rereading to check writing and remember meaning.

Laurie:	*Our* is a word we have been working on. We have written it a few times in our book about our neighborhood. It begins with that /ow/ sound. But what two letters make the /ow/ sound in *our*?
Student:	*O-u.*
Laurie:	Sometimes we have *o-w* like in *how*, but you are right that it is *o-u* in *our*.

A student comes up to write *ou*, but forgets to put a space between words. Laurie reminds the student that a space is needed here and covers the mistake with white tape. As the same student tries again, Laurie asks the class why a space is needed. They remember it is for a new word.

Laurie:	Now say that word again and listen for the sound at the end. [Students say *our* and call out *R*. The same student who wrote *ou* writes *r*.] That's a word we just need to know, especially because we are writing a book on OUR neighborhood, and we will write *our* often. Let's put that one on the word wall today.

She then quickly calls on three students to spell *our*. The student who wrote *our* leads the class in rereading.

NOTICE: For the last word (*neighborhood*), Laurie writes part of the word that is too hard *(neigh)* and teaches two spelling strategies: (1) break words into syllables to write them and (2) use what you know to help you spell a new word (e.g., *or* helps with *bor*). They also focus on the period at the end of the sentence.

Laurie: The last word in our sentence is a long word, so it helps to clap it out, like we have been practicing. Let's clap this word and then write each part.

The class claps *neigh*. Laurie writes "neigh" to represent the first syllable. The class claps *neigh-bor*.

Laurie: The second syllable has a word we know in it. The *b* is easy, so let me write that. Now what do we hear in that word? [Students talk about *or*.] That's a snap word for us, and it's in the middle of this longer word.

Laurie calls a student to write *or*. The class claps *neigh-bor-hood*. Students work on spelling *hood*. One student comes up and writes the whole syllable. They talk about hearing the /h/ and that /oo/ is like *school* although they can't really hear /oo/. They hear the /d/. The student who wrote *hood* leads the class in rereading.

Laurie: We finished our sentence. Show me what we need to tell our readers to stop. You can all write it in the air. [Students write a period in the air.] Jasmine, you really have been working on putting those periods at the end of your sentences. Can you please come up and write one for us?

Before they move on to Review, the class does two things:

1. Rereads the message while Jasmine points to each word.

2. Counts how many words they wrote.

The third example of Listen in on a Lesson features Pinnecko helping her fourth graders write one sentence in their opinion piece arguing that students should be encouraged to visit art museums.

LISTEN IN ON A LESSON: Grade 4

Experience

The students took a field trip to an art museum.

Prewrite

The students prepared to write an opinion paragraph about the importance of this trip to their principal. They brainstormed what to include in the paragraph and were reminded of opinion techniques such as including reasons and examples.

Every fourth grader should have a chance to go to the art museum. One reason is that learning outside of the classroom is interesting and exciting. We learned how art can tell a story. For example, we saw a painting of a girl who falls in love with a crusader, her father's enemy. *If you allow your students to go to an art museum, they will also learn about the feelings and emotions of an artist and how they express them in their artwork.* An example of this is when Pablo Picasso was in his "blue" period, he painted pictures using dark tones to express his depressed feelings and mood. These are the reasons why every fourth grader should have an opportunity to visit an art museum.

Opinion Writing (Grade 4)
(Italicized sentence is the focus of the Listen in on a Lesson)

Compose

The students wrote the paragraph over two days of interactive writing.

Share the Pen

One of the sentences written during that day's interactive writing session is "If you allow your students to go to an art museum, they will also learn about the feelings and emotions of an artist and how they express them in their artwork."

NOTICE: How the in-the-moment attention given to capitalization, commas, and homonyms was both relevant and authentic. The expectation was clear that students should incorporate these understandings into their own writing.

Pinnecko:	OK, we have decided on our sentence. We'll begin writing it up on our chart now. Alicia, you will be our first writer. You will write the first part of our sentence: "If you allow your students to go to an art museum." As Alicia comes up to the easel, let's think about those words. Anything we should make sure that Alicia keeps in mind as she writes?
Student:	Start with a capital! [The class laughs.]
Pinnecko:	Yes, that's right. I think most of you know that by now, but it's a good reminder!
Student:	Write neatly and put enough space between each word so that we can easily read it.
Pinnecko:	Yes—another good suggestion.
Student:	Don't mix up capital letters with lowercase letters.
Pinnecko:	I'm so glad you brought that up! I do notice that some of you like to throw in capital letters here and there in your writing. I know you know the difference between a capital *A* and a lowercase *a*. When you are writing a piece for school (or for something else that is important), be sure to follow the capitalization rules you know.

Alicia begins to write the first part of the sentence quickly.

Pinnecko:	Alicia, while you write, we are watching your handwriting and spacing very closely! Be sure you are thoughtful about capitalization and spacing.

Alicia slows for a moment to check her writing.

Pinnecko: So far, so good! Can someone quickly spell *museum*?

Student: *M-u-s-e-u-m.*

Pinnecko: Great—let's see if Alicia spelled it correctly. [Checks the word for correct spelling] Thanks, Alicia. This looks good. Alicia, can you lead us through what you just wrote? [Alicia points to each word as the students read it aloud.] OK, the next part of our sentence reads, "they will also learn about the feelings and emotions of an artist and how they express them in their artwork." Let's read the first part of the sentence together again and add in the second half, too.

Pinnecko guides her class to say the sentence aloud.

Pinnecko: I noticed that most of you paused for a quick moment after the word *museum*. Listen as I say the whole sentence again. Listen for the pause.

Pinnecko says the sentence again and pauses after the word *museum*.

Pinnecko: Did you hear the pause?

Students: Yes.

Pinnecko: Why is there a pause?

Student: Because the sentence is long, and you need a break.

Student: And it is kinda the beginning part of the sentence.

Pinnecko: Yes, you are both right. The first group of words is the beginning part of our sentence. We call it a sentence clause. And readers do need to pause when reading a longer sentence. The pause helps them to follow and understand the ideas. When we come to the end of a clause, we need to let readers know by including punctuation.

Student: A comma!

Pinnecko: Yes, we need a comma after the word *museum*. Alicia, can you add the comma into our writing?

Alicia adds the comma.

Pinnecko: Brian, can you come up and write the next part of our sentence? You will write the words "they will also learn about the feelings and emotions of an artist." Be sure your handwriting is readable and remember to use all lowercase letters in this part. Anything tricky we need to help Brian with?

Student: Might need to help with how to spell *emotions*.

Pinnecko: OK. Who knows that one?

Student: I do! *E-m-o-t-i-o-n-s*.

Pinnecko: Yep, that's it. Let's all spell it out loud. [The class spells *emotions* out loud.] When Brian gets to that word, let's all spell it aloud for him.

Brian begins writing.

Pinnecko: Everyone, let's look closely to see if all of his letters are lowercase. And, while he's writing, I wonder if you can also think quietly in your head about any other words you know that end like the word *emotion*. If you come up with one, give me a thumbs-up.

Several students give a thumbs-up sign. Brian writes the words without any errors. When he gets to the word *emotions*, he stops and waits.

Pinnecko: OK, let's spell it as Brian writes.

Students: *E-m-o-t-i-o-n-s*.

Pinnecko: Nice teamwork! Who can share a word that ends like *emotion*?

Different students quickly reply: *Imagination! Frustration! Situation! Vacation! Conversation!*

Pinnecko: Excellent. All of those words have the *-tion* ending, which we spell *t-i-o-n*. It's a very common suffix that you need to know and be able to spell. OK, Brian, can you lead us through the rereading of our sentence so far?

Brian cues the class to the beginning of the sentence and moves his finger along the text as the class reads what has been written so far.

Pinnecko: Nice job. We need one last writer for our sentence. Ricardo, come on up! You will finish up our sentence by writing, "and how they express them in their artwork."

Ricardo begins writing, and when he comes to the word *their*, he writes *there*. He then writes the remainder of the sentence and puts a period at the end.

Pinnecko: Let's take a look at our sentence. Ricardo, can you lead us in a rereading of the completed sentence?

The class rereads it.

Pinnecko: Does anyone notice any errors?

Student: I'm not sure he spelled *there* correctly.

Student: Yes, he did. He spelled it the right way.

Student: No, I mean I think it's the wrong *there*.

Student: I get so confused on which *there* to use when I write!

The students discussed and debated briefly about whether the intended word was spelled *there* or *their* or *they're*. Working with Pinnecko's support, the students helped one another figure out the different meanings and spellings of the word *their*. The students thought about the meaning of their sentence ("their artwork") and determined which form of the word was needed. Pinnecko then mentioned several other common homonyms that can cause confusion for writers, such as *to*, *too*, and *two* and *read* and *red*. Pinnecko wrapped up Share the Pen with the following guidance.

Pinnecko: Pay attention to these kinds of words—they're called homonyms—when you are writing your own pieces. Be sure to stop and think about the meaning of your sentence. This will help you select the correct form and spelling of the word. Nice work on this! Let's reread our whole piece one last time before we stop for today.

Finally, the last example highlights a lesson in Melissa's fifth-grade class in which the students are typing up their response to a prompt, "Describe the rock cycle," as a way of preparing for an upcoming standardized assessment.

LISTEN IN ON A LESSON: *Grade 5*

Experience

The students were studying rocks and minerals in their science class. As a way of preparing for an upcoming standardized assessment, the class responded to the prompt that asked them to describe the rock cycle.

Prewrite

Students used their notes and a graphic organizer to prepare for their writing.

Compose

The students wrote the piece over three days of interactive writing.

Share the Pen

One of the sentences written during one day's interactive writing session is "Sedimentary rocks are formed when sediments such as weathered rocks, sand, and dead organisms experience forceful pressure and are cemented into layers."

Rocking the Rock Cycle

The three types of rocks that make up Earth's crust are sedimentary, igneous, and metamorphic rocks. The Rock Cycle forms these rocks which come in diverse shapes, colors, and sizes. *Sedimentary rocks are formed when sediments such as weathered rocks, sand, and dead organisms experience forceful pressure and are cemented into layers.* Sedimentary rocks transform into metamorphic rock when the rock encounters extreme heat and pressure. Igneous rocks are created when magma, or molten rock, cools and solidifies. A process that morphs igneous rocks into sediment is called weathering and erosion. Igneous rocks can mutate into metamorphic rocks when they undergo a great amount of heat and pressure. Metamorphic rocks are created from igneous and sedimentary rocks that have been exposed to an extravagant amount of heat and pressure. The melting process alters metamorphic rocks by changing them into magma, while weathering and erosion deconstruct metamorphic rocks into sediment. The Rock Cycle includes numerous processes that form and modify Earth's crust.

Interactive Writing in Science (Grade 5)
(Italicized sentence is the focus of the Listen in on a Lesson)

Paper Keyboards for Individual Students

Student Types on Paper Keyboard (Grade 5)

Student Shares the Keyboard (Grade 5)

Ahead of the lesson, Melissa made paper keyboards for her students. These keyboards allowed all students to be engaged with the important typing and formatting issues that writers face.

Melissa: Now that we have our sentence ready, let's begin to type. Tiffany, you will get us started. Come on up and please type: "Sedimentary rocks are formed when sediments."

Tiffany: How do I make it go in?

Melissa: Ask me that again using more specific language so I can understand.

Tiffany: How do I make the writing go in...like for a paragraph?

Melissa: Great question. When you type on the keyboard, we call that using the Tab button. It's here.

Melissa shows Tiffany where the Tab button is and how to use it. Tiffany continues typing.

Melissa: While Tiffany types for us, use your keyboard to practice how you hit Tab to indent. Then go ahead and practice the same typing that Tiffany is doing.

Tiffany finishes her words. Here's what she has written: "Sedimenrey rocks are from when sedimens."

Melissa: OK, let's all look at what Tiffany typed. Notice that there are some red squiggly lines under some of her words. What does that mean?

Student: She spelled something wrong.

Melissa: That is true. When you see a red line under your word that means that the computer doesn't recognize it as a word. Most of the time this means it is misspelled. So what should she do?

Student: Look it up in the dictionary.

Student: We can find that word on our Word Wall.

Melissa: Yes, those are great suggestions. Let me show another way.

Word Wall in Math and Science (Grade 5)

Student:	Oh, I know. She should use spell-check. It's faster!
Melissa:	Yes, exactly! Spell-check is a helpful tool that Microsoft Word has for correcting spelling errors. Here's how it works. [Melissa shows students how they can click on the word and suggested spellings appear.] Tiffany, check each of the red underlined words to see if you can fix the spelling.

Tiffany corrects *sedimentary* and *sediments*. The typing now reads, "Sedimentary rocks are from when sediments."

Melissa:	Let's read what Tiffany typed.

The class rereads and discovers that *formed* is not spelled correctly.

Melissa:	Why didn't a red squiggly line appear on the word *from*?
Student:	Because it is a real word.
Student:	But it isn't what we meant. We wanted the word *formed*.
Melissa:	You are both right. The computer recognizes the word *from*, and it technically does make sense in the phrase so far. But it isn't what WE meant. We did mean to write *formed*. How can Tiffany fix this?
Student:	It should be *f-o-r-m-e-d*.
Melissa:	Yep, that's it. Tiffany, go ahead and fix that spelling.

Melissa [to the whole class while Tiffany types]: So even though spell-check is a very helpful tool, it doesn't work for every error. If you accidentally write a similar word or when you misspell one word and it turns into another word...the computer won't catch that spelling mistake for you. So you will still always need to reread your writing. When we reread what Tiffany typed, we discovered our error. OK, I need Tyree up here next. Tyree, you will write "such as weathered rocks, sand, and dead organisms." While Tyree types, all of you need to do the same on your keyboards.

Melissa: Tyree, when you write, be sure to slow down with the word *organisms* and sound out each syllable.

Tyree types the following: "such as wethered rocks sand and dead orgenisms."

Melissa: OK, Tyree, take a look at your typing. Anything you want to try and fix on your own?

Tyree: I will fix the spelling words. I know how to use spell-check.

Melissa: Great, go ahead and do this now. While he does this, I want the rest of you to line your fingers up on the following keys. Put your left pinky on the letter *A*...then put your left ring finger on *S* and then your left middle finger on *D* and your left pointer finger on *F*. Your left thumb can rest on the space bar. Now do this same thing with your right hand—put your right pinky on the key that has a colon and a semicolon on it... [Melissa shows her students the "home keys" for efficient typing. She explains to her students how these can help them become faster at typing.] When you practice typing at your desk or when you type at home, trying using this method. Try it now as you "paper type" from the beginning of our piece.

Students type on their practice keyboards.

Melissa: OK, Tyree, how are you doing?

Tyree: I corrected the spelling.

Melissa [refocuses the whole class again]: Let's all look at what our sentence says so far. Let's reread it together. [The class rereads it.] Anything we need to add or fix?

She pauses and waits. No one responds.

Melissa: Let's look closely at what our sentence is saying. We are describing how sedimentary rocks are formed. We then mention three types of sediments: weathered rocks, sand, and dead organisms. We have a list of three specific sediments. What should we include when we are writing a list? Think for a moment. What writing rule do you know about from your ELA class? I know you have practiced this before.

Student:	Oh yeah ... we need a comma!!
Melissa:	Where?
Student:	After each one of our list items.
Melissa:	Yes, that's right. Tyree, look at the three types of sediments. Can you go back and insert a comma after each one of these sediments? You will need to use the Insert key so that you don't delete all of your writing. Do you know how to use this key?
Tyree:	No.
Melissa:	No problem, let me show you. [Says to the class] While I'm walking Tyree through this, go back and practice typing with the home keys method I just showed you.

Students go back to typing on their paper keyboards. Melissa shows Tyree how to use the Insert key to add the necessary commas. She also addresses the spacing issue with him. Then she brings the whole class together to reread the sentence so far.

Melissa:	Tyree and I also fixed some spacing issues. Be careful when you type to hit the spacebar only once between each word. We need to finish up this sentence quickly. James, come on up and finish it for us. You will type: "experience forceful pressure and are cemented into layers." While James types this, the rest of you type it as well. Keep trying to use the home key method.

James types, "experience forceful pressure and are cement into layers."

Melissa:	Take a look, everyone. No squiggly lines this time. So are we all set?
Students:	Yes?!
Melissa:	Are you sure?? I don't think so... [The class laughs.] How will we know for sure?
Student:	We need to reread our writing.
Melissa:	Yes! Let's reread what has been typed. [When they reread they discover the grammar error in the word *cement*.] So the lesson to remember here is that you must always reread your writing—whether it is handwritten or typed—to see if it makes sense. The computer won't catch that for you. Let's fix the word *cement* so that our sentence makes sense. Then we will stop for today. [Melissa leads the class as they reread the entire piece so far.] OK, we are making great progress. I will save our work before closing the program.

WHAT TEACHERS ARE SAYING

I like that I can spend time on conventions. As a math and science teacher I often feel so content-driven. But addressing conventions is important for my students.   —Melissa (Grade 5)

Challenges of Share the Pen

As we have noted earlier, there are many things happening during Share the Pen. As you can imagine, the work it takes to engage both a single student and the entire class thoughtfully around conventions is demanding. It is during this phase that classroom management can "make or break" the lesson. Pacing becomes critical, as you must keep all students with you. In Chapter 9, we suggest tips for routines, materials, and scheduling that will support your classroom management.

Another challenge is that many decisions must be made rather quickly during this phase. Knowing the right convention to highlight, the appropriate student to select for sharing the pen, and the ways in which to engage your entire class around the convention being addressed requires quick in-the-moment thinking. As mentioned, with time and practice these decisions will become more comfortable and predictable for you and the students.

Planning for Share the Pen

By this point in the lesson, many of your *planning* decisions have already been made. The piece has a clear purpose and the sentence has been composed. You have focused on craft and considered the appropriate length and complexity of the text. When you plan for Share the Pen, there are two additional planning areas to consider.

Differentiated Instruction

Just like in Compose, knowing which students to engage during Share the Pen is essential. Again, plan for this ahead of time by reading students' independent writing frequently. Take notice of the students who struggle with particular conventions such as spelling, punctuation, or handwriting. Also, pay attention to patterns and trends that exist for groups of students. Consider who may be ready and capable of writing a large amount of text and who might contribute something smaller. This data informs those in-the-moment decisions of how and where you might break up the sentence to be written (or whether you will select a student to write the entire sentence). Your advanced planning allows you to differentiate your instruction efficiently and keep the momentum going.

Consider Your Materials for Share the Pen

The materials needed for Share the Pen must be prepared and organized before the lesson begins. This advanced planning allows you to focus on the instructional priorities rather than on logistics. First, you decide whether you will be writing or typing the piece. If you opt to write with a pen or marker,

Table 14 Materials to Consider for Share the Pen

Options	Materials
Share the Pen (Without Technology)	• Easel or board centrally located • *White* paper or sentence strips • Lined sentence strips for emergent writers (solid base/top line, dotted middle line) • Lined chart paper with a more narrow width for more fluent writers • *Black* permanent marker • Correction tape or white paper and tape for correcting errors • Scissors (for PreK and K if you will cut sentence into words) • Grades 3–5: Individual writing space/tool for students to use as they practice conventions (e.g., small whiteboards, clipboards, lined paper with plastic sleeve)
Share the Pen (With Technology)	• Interactive whiteboard • *Black* stylus or marker for interactive whiteboard • 8.5″ × 11″ white lined paper appropriate for grade level and document camera
Share the Keyboard	• Computer or tablet located centrally and linked with LCD projector • Well-positioned screen • Individual "keyboards" (laminated) for students to practice typing
All Methods	• Name chart and alphabet chart (PreK–2) • Small marker board and black marker (for you to model) • Pointer to point to words for rereading (PreK–2)

select the most appropriate paper and writing tool. There are several options for this. The paper you use should be mounted on an easel or board in order to make the physical act of writing easier for students. You might also decide to write using technology, such as an interactive whiteboard or a document camera. Table 14 describes these different approaches and lists the materials to consider ahead of time.

If you decide to share a keyboard, you need to have the computer on with the blank document open and ready as soon as the lesson begins. Further, the computer should be located centrally so that you can simultaneously engage the class and support the individual student typing. Regardless of the specific materials you select, the overarching planning requirement is to make sure your materials are ready to go before the day's lesson begins.

Final Thoughts

Share the Pen is an instructionally rich part of an interactive writing lesson. During this phase, you emphasize the teaching of conventions as one student writes or types a portion of the sentence. You provide in-the-moment support for the student writing while engaging the entire class around that same principle. There are many teaching moves to navigate during Share the

Pen, and this phase changes as students grow as writers. Conventions naturally become more complex, the text to be written will be longer, and keyboarding becomes an option to include. Keeping the momentum going during this phase with so many decisions on your mind and all of your students to engage can be challenging. However, with thoughtful planning and repeated practice, these challenges can be overcome. Share the Pen offers an authentic guided writing experience focused on conventions. It is a valuable learning opportunity for your student writers.

CHAPTER 7

Review

Bringing a lesson to a thoughtful close requires skill and pacing! Review is where this occurs. Consider the following questions: How do you wrap up the lesson in an efficient and meaningful way? How do you help students connect this group writing experience with the work they will do independently?

After the message is complete, it is time to bring closure to the lesson in a purposeful way. Review is the step where this happens. In less than three minutes, two important teaching moves occur. First, the teacher asks students to continue interacting with the message to find examples of the principles taught during the lesson. This allows the students to revisit a few of the instructional points emphasized. After these points have been highlighted, the teacher briefly summarizes what has been learned about the craft and conventions of writing and then reminds students how this collaborative work should inform their own independent writing.

This chapter is much shorter than Compose and Share the Pen. In its brevity, it mirrors the actual phase of the lesson. However, the chapter will teach you how to revisit the skills and strategies that were practiced during an interactive writing lesson and will describe why Review is a critical step to include.

Review: Bringing the Lesson to a Close

At this point in the lesson, you and your students have been working hard on both craft and conventions. The piece is either complete or has reached an appropriate point for pausing (knowing that you will pick up where you left off in your next interactive writing session). It is now time to highlight the important teaching and learning that occurred while the piece was planned, composed, and written.

Review begins as you guide your students to interact with the piece once again. You ask them to find examples of the key principles taught during

WHAT TEACHERS ARE SAYING

Review is fast and fun. My students feel engaged in a writing scavenger hunt, and I know I am ending the lesson by hitting home some major teaching points. —Amy (Kindergarten)

the lesson. This allows students to revisit a few of the salient instructional points emphasized. For example, you might ask a student to come up and find a word that ends with the suffix -*ing*, a word with a capital letter, or the more interesting word they chose to write in place of *happy*. Or you might ask students to turn and talk to their neighbor about where you opted to use an exclamation point rather than a period in order to show readers your enthusiasm.

Next, you summarize for students what was learned during the lesson. For example, you might say something like, "Today we used a question for our lead. It was a good choice because it will immediately get our audience interested in our writing. We also focused on adding -*ed* to words to show the story already happened." You use the opportunity of having a text with which all students are deeply familiar to reinforce key writing principles. Finally, you remind students that they need to use these same skills and principles in their own independent writing.

Review: Making Time for Closure

Including some type of lesson wrap-up or closure is a commonly held practice among teachers. Initially considered the time in the lesson for summing up the key points, closure has evolved over the years and is often linked with two powerful teaching moves aligned with effective instruction: checking for understanding and teaching for transfer (e.g., Fisher & Frey, 2007a; Hunter, 1982; Marzano, 2007; Popham, 2008; Schmoker, 2011; Wolfe, 2011).

When thinking about interactive writing, closure is the time to revisit key points of a lesson, summarize the important concepts that were practiced, notice whether students are understanding these big ideas fully, and connect the learning to their independent writing. And yet, after the last punctuation mark is written and the text is reread one last time, you might be inclined to stop there, skip any closure, and move on to the next part of your day. While we are sensitive to the many demands on your time and on students' waning energy level after an intense lesson, we encourage you to incorporate this last quick but powerful step into your interactive writing routine.

Review allows you to wrap up your lesson in a way that is both energizing and fast-paced. You and your students can be excited about the piece and will celebrate the collective work that was done. Review also gives you one last chance to summarize and showcase the important craft and convention work you did as a community of writers. These teaching principles are then connected back to individual writers as you reinforce your expectation that students use these same skills and techniques in their own independent work. In these final moments, it is time to step back from the day's work in order to pull together the metacognitive experience for your students. Talk about the writing processes you practiced and use the piece as a tool for learning more about words and writing.

For example, you might say, "As we worked on our piece, we spent some time thinking of how to begin writing about the assembly performance in a creative and unique way—so that our readers would know *we* were the writers. We tried out some different phrases. We decided to say, 'Now, do you want to know about how our awesome and amazing spring concert began?' This sentence really captures our voice. It sounds like us! When you are writing on your own, you need to do this too. Think about how you would say something in your unique voice. Think about how your readers will know that *you* wrote it." This direct link back to your students' independent writing is an explicit teaching move. It solidifies their knowledge and ensures a higher rate of transfer to their own writing.

The Language and Sequence of Review

During Review, you discuss the piece in order to reinforce and summarize the craft and conventions that hold the most instructional value for your students. The first part of Review is interactive as you ask students to notice the details of their writing. In the second part, you summarize the learning by making final comments about the teaching points and accomplishments of the day's lesson and connecting it back to your students' own writing.

Part 1: An Interactive Study of Words and Writing

Review begins with one or two minutes of a quick-moving and engaging "word and writing study." You choose several specific features you want your students to find in the text written that day. For example, you might ask a question about punctuation and then choose a student to tap the punctuation on the actual text while the other students look on and give a thumbs-up for approval. There are many possible points to highlight within a piece. Select only the most relevant points to review on the basis of the work you did with students.

Student Finds the First Word in the Sentence During Review (PreK)

Student Finds the Word That Ends Like "Christopher" (Kindergarten)

Some teachers lead their students through this part of Review in a game-like or scavenger-hunt fashion. Again, your goal is to draw students' attention to some memorable examples of craft and conventions. Your students come to know that this activity signals the closure of the interactive writing lesson. Maximize this time to recognize and honor the thinking that was done collectively to write the piece. This will be a gratifying opportunity to engage one last time with what they wrote.

For the youngest writers who are newly developing their understanding of reading and writing, Review is a wonderful time to reinforce foundational understandings about the way print works. By revisiting a text that is accessible and readable by all, your students can practice what they are learning, especially about the mechanics of writing. That said, craft still holds a central place in instruction during interactive writing, especially during Compose. However, the first part of Review for emergent writers focuses primarily on conventions. The repetition of the fundamental understanding about concepts of print and basic conventions is valuable (Roth, 2009). Table 15 gives language you can use with your students to help them review teaching points about craft *and* conventions, including spelling, punctuation, concepts about print, or handwriting.

The teaching of conventions remains important for older writers as well. However, because older students write longer and more complex texts, the teaching emphasis around organization, word choice, sentence fluency, and voice grows and intensifies. During Review, it is essential that the teaching points around craft are explicitly highlighted for your students. Table 16 reflects a balance of both the craft and convention principles you might review with your students at this point in the lesson.

Part 2: A Summary of Key Points Covered in the Lesson

In the second part of Review, you close the lesson by naming the craft and convention principles emphasized in this lesson. Think of this as a one- or two-sentence summary to help your students consolidate what they learned. Further, you explicitly guide them again in linking their learning in this group lesson to what you expect them to do in their own writing. For example, "Today, we were very careful about putting a space between each of our words just like you need to do in your own writing" or "In this piece, we were very

Table 15 Possible Language for Review (Grades PreK–2)

Craft	*Can you find...* • A place where we used an interesting word OR a place where we thought really hard about choosing the best word? • Our title, the greeting of our letter, or (other organizational features)? • A place where we took two ideas and combined them into one long sentence? • A place where we took a big idea and broke it into two separate sentences? (applies in grades 1 and 2 only)
Spelling	*Can you find...* • A specific high-frequency ("snap") word? • A word that rhymes with... / sounds like...? • A word with (e.g., 1, 2, more than 2...) syllables? • A word with a specific spelling pattern (e.g., consonant cluster, vowel combination)? • A word that can be spelled another way but sounds the same (e.g., *to*, *two*, *too*)? • A compound word? • A contraction? • A word that ends with *-ing*, *-ed*, *-er*, or *s* to make it more than one? • A word with a silent letter? • A word that begins like... (e.g., *the*)?
Punctuation	*Can you find...* • A period (question mark, exclamation point) and tell us why we used it?
Concepts About Print	*Can you count...* • The number of words we wrote? • How many sentences we wrote? *Can you find...* • The letter... (e.g., select the letter that students worked on in the piece)? • A capital or lowercase letter? • Where we began the message? • The beginning of the sentence? • The end of the sentence?
Handwriting	*Can you find...* • A place where we used a "tall letter" ("short letter" or "letter that goes below the line")? • A place where we worked on how to write a letter (a place where a mistake occurred)?

thoughtful about providing clear evidence to support each topic sentence. Make sure you do this when you write your piece."

This final step should feel like an energy boost as students' attention shifts away from the details of the piece toward a more holistic view of what they did as writers and how it applies to their own writing lives. If the piece will be continued in another interactive writing session, you summarize by connecting today's work to the work planned for future sessions by saying something like, "We will continue this piece and focus on... (e.g., the middle of our story, our second argument, providing more evidence, another fact we learned)."

Table 16 Possible Language for Review, Grades 2–5

Craft	*Who can remind the class how we...* • Organized our piece (e.g., paragraphs, numbered list)? • Thought about our lead ("hooked" our readers)? • Ended our piece? • Used titles and headings? • Included transition words for time flow (e.g., *then, after, because of this, the next day, finally*)? • Structured our writing (e.g., compare/contrast, sequence, problem/solution)? • Avoided "overused" words (e.g., *happy, fun, like, said*)? • Included strong verbs? • Used memorable language: vivid, striking, or unexpected words? • Described through "showing vs. telling"? • Incorporated a variety of simple and complex sentences? • Expressed our ideas/information in a unique and surprising way? • Used punctuation (ellipses, dashes, end marks) to interest and engage our audience?
Conventions	*Where did we...* • Slow down to think about the spelling of a "tricky" word (e.g., a multisyllabic word, unique vocabulary word)? • Pay attention to an important grammar rule (e.g., subject/verb agreement, noun/pronoun agreement, prepositional phrases, adjectives, adverbs, contractions, plurals)? • Need to think about the tense of our verbs (past, present, or future)? • Practice important capitalization rules for 　○ Proper nouns (days of week, months, cities, states, names of people and specific places)? 　○ Titles, headings, subheadings? 　○ First word of sentence? • Consider the best end mark for a sentence (i.e., period, exclamation point, or question mark)? • Include unique punctuation in order to clarify or enhance the meaning of our piece (e.g., quotation marks, commas, ellipses, dashes, apostrophes, periods after abbreviations)? • Practice letter formation/handwriting? • Discuss important keyboarding skills (ctrl, shift, tab, caps lock, delete/insert)? • Practice word-processing skills (saving a document, uploading, sending attachments)?

How Review Changes Over Time

Unlike other phases in the interactive writing lesson (e.g., Prewrite, Compose, and Share the Pen), Review holds the same structure and pacing across all grades, PreK–5. It is consistently a brief but significant closure that includes an opportunity for your students to revisit the text to focus on a few memorable points of instruction and a final summary by you. The teaching points, as noted in previous chapters, become more complex and sophisticated. For example, a PreK student might be asked to find a capital letter, the period at the end of the sentence, or the spaces between two words, whereas a fourth grader might point out the transition words that tie the paragraph together, a specific quote used as evidence, or the phrase written in a unique way to convey enthusiasm.

As expected, the summary may be simpler for younger students, as only one or two key points would be highlighted. For older students, two or three points are generally the norm. Overall, the language and sequence of Review stay the same, as does the length of time it takes.

Planning for Review

The teaching that occurs during Review is organic, and there is much room for spontaneous discovery. Although you can anticipate the time to highlight key learnings about craft and conventions, you will not know the exact plan for this until the sentence is crafted and the writing complete. However, your decisions about what to call out will, as always, be informed by your students' work, the curriculum, and what you know about good writing. Your teaching decisions are *always* about the instructional needs of your students.

Final Thoughts

Review is a short yet powerful part of the interactive writing lesson. You and your students have created and written a common text that holds relevance and meaning for everyone. During Review, you take advantage of this investment by using the written piece to revisit key writing points that arose throughout the lesson. Students engage actively with the text by searching for the memorable examples of craft and conventions. This experience solidifies their learning. Review brings initial closure to the lesson when you summarize the key learning points and remind students to transfer these same principles into their own writing.

CHAPTER 8

Extend

Now is the time to reap the benefits of your students' hard work! An interactive writing piece is most meaningful when it is extended in strategic ways. How can you use the completed interactive writing piece to support and advance students' literacy development?

During Extend, the class continues to use the completed writing piece as an instructional tool. For example, the teacher might mount the writing to make a class book or mural that students can reread regularly or share the writing with the intended audience. Students may also write similar pieces on their own and use the piece as a helpful exemplar of the genre. Students in primary grades often illustrate final pieces with collages, photographs, or other forms of art that match the style of writing.

In this chapter, you will learn about many interesting and creative ways a piece can be stretched. Extending an interactive writing piece can influence your students' literacy development positively in multiple ways. When you optimize Extend, you motivate your student writers, deepen their reading and writing knowledge, and, ultimately, propel their independent writing forward.

Extend: The What

The pieces written during interactive writing are, in and of themselves, valuable artifacts of your teaching and your students' learning. During Extend, you widen and deepen their influence on students' literacy development. Extending a piece can happen in myriad ways. Extensions can be brief activities lasting just a few minutes or one writing period. Or they can be longer, requiring several days or weeks to complete.

In this chapter, we include photographs that capture both the breadth and the depth of different extensions—what you do with your class *after* the writing is complete. As you browse the photos of interactive writing included in this chapter and throughout the book, you see that different options

> ## WHAT TEACHERS ARE SAYING
>
> I start my classroom each year with almost blank walls and quickly fill them with pieces created during interactive writing lessons. The pieces make the space rich with print that is authentic and meaningful for every student. The students literally read the walls, and we are all proud of the beauty we have created. —Katie (Grade 1)

for extending a piece serve different purposes and outcomes. In all cases, the extensions support and advance students' reading and writing.

Notice that many examples include art; however, please understand that extensions do not need to be extravagant projects requiring extensive supplies and materials. They can be simple and straightforward. The true beauty will come through as you and your students take time to focus on presentation and when the final display is mounted thoughtfully and arranged neatly. Hopefully these suggestions will inspire you as you think more about the why and how of Extend.

Extend: The Why

After the interactive writing piece has been completed and reviewed, you may be inclined to leave the writing piece on the easel or click on Save and place the document into a folder on your computer. It might seem that you have done enough. You and your students planned, crafted, revised, and edited a piece of writing. You then reviewed the key learning that took place. However, if you think back to Chapter 2, the final phase of the writing process is *publishing*.

When we share our writing with others or use it for its intended purpose, we complete the process that all writers go through. You and your students discussed and practiced many important writing skills and strategies as you moved through the lesson. Extend is the way to lift the learning to a higher level. It also can be a moment for celebration as you step back and look at the finished piece.

Your students feel connected to this writing, so doing more with the piece is well worth the time. When you opt to extend a piece, you reinforce the previous work you and your students completed during the lesson. Further, there is *new* learning that can occur for them. Extensions can celebrate and affirm your student writers, contribute to a print-rich classroom environment, and provide a timely opportunity for students to take the important skills and strategies practiced during the lesson and apply them to their own writing.

WHAT TEACHERS ARE SAYING

By the end, they see what they have created. They are invested in the piece. —Sonja (Grade 4)

Celebrate and Affirm Student Writers

The piece you and your students completed during interactive writing took focus and hard work. It is opportune to celebrate this accomplishment by displaying it or sharing it with others in authentic ways. Taking time to do this sends a clear message: What we write is meant to be read! And when you "publish" your piece, you reinforce the idea that presentation matters. Students want their work to look finished and polished when others see it. Rather than displaying commercially made posters or pictures, your classroom's walls become filled with original student writing that celebrates the community of writers within it.

Celebrating and affirming student writers holds a particularly important role for struggling writers. We hear time and again about the student who is reluctant to complete writing assignments or who panics when faced with the blank page. These students often dread the writing period because they do not believe they can produce a piece worth reading. When they see a finished piece thoughtfully mounted, displayed, and perhaps enhanced with illustrations or photographs, *and* they know they had a role in its creation, they realize that their ideas *are* worth reading!

To be clear, all students will benefit from the celebration of the finished piece. An interesting observation we have made is that when students know finished pieces are *always* displayed or used in meaningful ways, they have high expectations for their interactive writing and are deeply invested in the lesson. Creating something of high-quality that represents their collective efforts is empowering for them. Moreover, when students see the real-world purpose of their piece, their confidence grows as they view themselves as capable authors who use writing in a variety of meaningful ways.

Contribute to a Print-Rich Classroom Environment

A Student "Reads Around the Room" (Grades PreK–1)

In classrooms focused on literacy learning, there are many resources available that support students' independent reading and writing (Pinnell & Fountas, 1998). Completed interactive writing pieces work well in this regard. They are powerful resources that hold instructional value for students. For example, students may reread the pieces using a pointer during "Read Around the Room" or use the pieces to search for specific words in "Write Around the Room," two activities embedded into independent practice time or centers. If your final piece is a book, bind and place it into the reading area for students to select for independent reading.

If you and your students have typed the piece through Share the Keyboard, you can enlarge the font, print the piece, and display it on a writing bulletin board that grows as the year progresses. Students can also use the displayed pieces throughout the year as models for when they write in similar genres.

One of the best parts of our work as literacy coaches is being able to visit many schools and classrooms. When we enter a classroom that is filled with meaningful student work displayed attractively, we see the unique footprint of literacy learning that students have completed over time. Interactive writing pieces are especially powerful artifacts for visitors (e.g., parents, administrators, colleagues) to see as they walk through your room, drop by for a moment, or observe your teaching. These displays are concrete examples of the writing work your students have experienced.

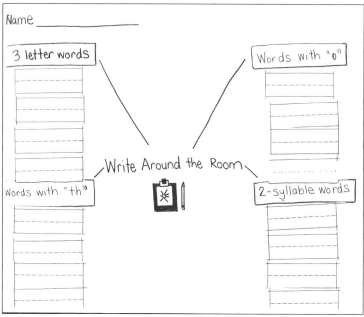

An example of "Write Around the Room" (Grade 1)

Moreover, when the pieces are displayed neatly and thoughtfully, the environment feels welcoming and productive for your students, too. It becomes an authentic place for students to think and write!

Provide a Timely Opportunity for Students to Apply Craft and Convention Strategies to Their Own Writing

Another powerful rationale for Extend is the timely opportunity it provides for students to apply the exact craft and convention techniques practiced during the lesson to their own writing. As we discussed in Chapter 2, students need many different types of writing experiences across their days and weeks in order to develop and grow. Interactive writing works best when it is a slice of your writing program nested between teacher modeling and independent practice. Thus, an intentional link must be made between the interactive writing work and what students do on their own.

Imagine a swimmer who has just learned how to do the breaststroke sequence by working closely with the swim coach and finally feels what it means to pull, breathe, kick, and glide. It would be a lost opportunity if that swimmer hopped out of the pool and did not return until the next week's lesson. Rather, it is far more helpful if the coach pauses, reminds the swimmer of what she just did, and tells her to try it now on her own. Timing matters. Having just experienced success with the support of the coach, the swimmer is primed to try it out by herself.

This analogy connects well with interactive writing. If, during your lesson, students learned about putting space between their words, they are ready now to try that on their own. If students learned how to combine short sentences into one longer one, have them see if there are places where this can work in their own writing. Or if a focus in the lesson was on features of a specific genre, have students write a similar piece independently.

The familiar saying, "Strike while the iron is hot" fits here. This does *not* mean that independent writing time must follow the group time immediately. Instead, we advocate for offering students other times during the day and week to write on their own. During these moments of independence, you guide your students to apply what they are learning from their interactive writing experiences.

Your finished piece will have many skills and strategies worth highlighting for students. Remember, however, that your students have a range of needs and can take on only so much at a time. Individualizing some of the guidance you give by matching which skill or strategy fits best with a particular writer may help. This differentiated approach ensures that students are taking on what they are truly capable of owning themselves. In the end, use the interactive writing *process* to affirm students and to propel them forward as capable writers.

Extend: The How

The big question to ask yourself for Extend is, "Now what will we do with it?" Thinking about extensions in four broad categories helps.

1. Analyze the Piece

The piece you and your students have created is filled with teaching opportunities. Revisiting the piece is well worth your time. Students benefit from this repeated exposure as they work on fluency, concepts of print, and new vocabulary. Using the piece as an exemplar for a particular writing genre is quite helpful if students are expected to do this type of writing on their own. Further, reinforcing the craft and convention elements practiced during the lesson is critical if you want your students to apply these independently.

2. Incorporate Visuals

Illustrations often complete the message of the piece. Visuals support emergent readers in focusing on meaning. For more complex writing, illustrations can enhance and provide vivid images for readers to appreciate.

Charts, graphs, diagrams, and tables provide visual data when writing in math and science. Often, there are more extensive illustrations with interactive writing for younger students. These visual supports typically decrease as the gradient of text becomes more challenging. This natural shift reflects the developmental needs of readers who rely progressively less on picture support for comprehension. Incorporating visuals does not require artistic expertise! Using photographs, cut-outs from magazines, or online images and most certainly harnessing students' creative talent can bring visual life to the writing.

3. Highlight the Piece's Real-World Purpose

Sharing the piece with its intended audience confirms that the writing holds an authentic purpose. This happens when the piece is reread during independent work time or centers or when it is displayed in a place where many can read and appreciate it. Specific types of writing like letters or e-mails can be sent to their intended recipient. In all cases, these types of extensions highlight the real-world purpose that writing holds beyond the easel or computer screen.

4. Connect the Piece to Students' Independent Writing

Your students benefit greatly when the piece is used as a launching pad for their own writing. You might opt for them to write a new ending for the piece, the next chapter, or a piece that is similar. Alternatively, you might ask students to take on a particular craft or convention strategy that came up in the interactive writing lesson. These extensions reinforce the overarching goal for interactive writing: to positively influence your students' independent work.

As you see in Table 17, within these four categories there are many specific types of extensions to consider. Also notice that different extensions promote different learning opportunities. Your goal, as always, is to advance students' literacy development. Therefore, selecting the best options for your particular students is essential.

On the pages that follow, we show a collection of interactive writing pieces with a range of extensions. In each example, we highlight the interactive writing that was done collaboratively and the way or ways the piece was extended. As you review these photographs, notice the wide variety of extensions and how they each support and advance students' literacy development. Also, notice how Extend changes over time. In the primary-grade samples, you will see visuals incorporated through photos, drawings, and painting. You will also see creative displays of these pieces.

Table 17 How Extend Supports and Advances Students' Literacy Development

Analyze the Piece Continually		
• Reread the piece as a shared reading activity.	→	Students work on fluency.
• Reread and highlight the high-frequency words (PreK–2).	→	Students practice reading and spelling high-frequency words.
• Add any new/interesting words used in the piece to the Word Wall.	→	Students practice and learn new vocabulary.
• Practice concepts of print (e.g., cut apart the sentence word by word in order to teach the concept of word).	→	Students continue to work on concepts of print.
• Highlight the genre features.	→	Students learn the key features of a particular genre.
Incorporate Visuals		
• Draw simple illustrations and/or sketches. • Add more elaborate artwork (painting, collage, or other appropriate medium). • Include photographs, charts, or graphs that connect to the writing. • If the piece is in response to a text, replicate the illustrator's style in your own illustrations.	→	• Visuals and text together create a complete message for students to understand. • Readers use visuals as support for reading. • Visuals provide detail and accuracy, which enhance the message or content of the writing.
Highlight the Piece's Real-World Purpose		
• Share the piece with the intended audience. • Reread the piece (turn it into a book for the class library, include it during independent reading or as part of "read the room," etc.). • Display the piece (within the classroom, hallway, somewhere within the school, etc.). • Use the writing for its designed function (list of rules, signs, "how-to's," directions, etc.).	→	• Students use/read the piece in relevant ways (read the book or chart during independent reading, use the information for tasks, follow the directions, etc.). • Students see themselves as real authors who write for real-world purposes.
Connect to Students' Independent Writing		
• Write a similar piece following a similar format. • Extend the piece (write what happens next, write a new ending, write their own version, etc.). • Incorporate one or more of the craft and/or convention elements that was practiced into their own writing.	→	• Students apply the craft and convention strategies practiced in the lesson in a timely way when they independently write a new version or continue on with the piece.

As writers develop, it may become less important for visuals to be incorporated and more important for the class piece to serve as a genre exemplar that informs students' independent writing. Because these pieces may be typed or written in conventionally sized print, displaying them on bulletin boards is less common. Rather, students might receive a copy of the piece to keep in their writing folders for future reference. What *is* common throughout these examples is how the teachers considered a genuine purpose and audience for the writing. This is an extension that holds throughout all grades.

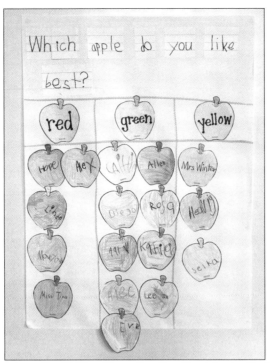

Interactive Writing Piece: *Question About Apples (PreK)*

Extension: *Students did a taste test and recorded the results on an apple graph.*

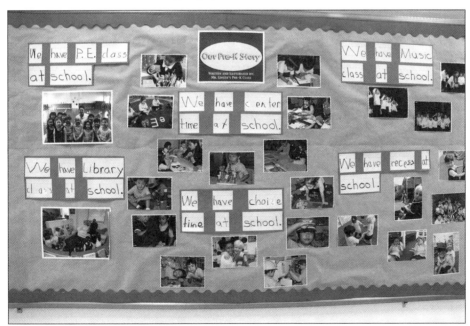

Interactive Writing Piece: *Our PreK Story (PreK)*

Extensions: *(1) Students incorporated photographs of themselves at the different activities, and (2) the piece was displayed on a bulletin board outside the classroom.*

Interactive Writing Piece: *Excerpt From a Class Book Titled "Our Field Trip to the Zoo" (PreK)*

Extensions: *(1) Students illustrated each page with watercolor paintings and photographs of the animal, and (2) the piece was displayed as a book on the wall.*

Interactive Writing Piece: *Sentence About Sinterklaas (PreK)*

Extension: *The teacher printed an image of this text for each student and they created their unique illustrations to match the writing.*

During Interactive Writing (IW) we start by thinking of an idea together as a group and then we take turns in writing the words, part of the words and supplying punctuation. Then the children reread what we have written to check and make sure that the writing can be understood. We do IW at least three times per week. This is a sample of the work we do together:

This week we also learned about the short sound of vowel "Oo" and the middle sound it makes in words like dog, cot, mop, pop, jog, and more. Me made fun dog paper puppets.

Interactive Writing Piece: *Book About Healthy Choices (Kindergarten)*

Extensions: *(1) The students illustrated each page, (2) the book was displayed on a hallway bulletin board, and (3) the teacher photographed the piece and included it in a family newsletter that highlighted the interactive writing approach.*

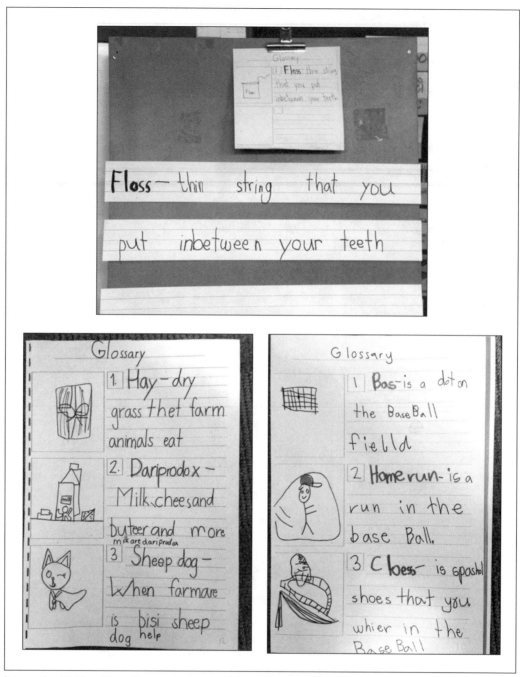

Interactive Writing Piece: *Glossary Entry About Dental Floss (Kindergarten)*

Extension: *Students included a glossary when they wrote their own "All About Books."*

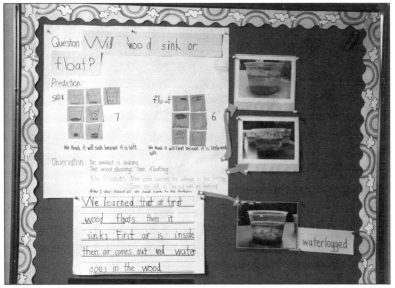

Interactive Writing Piece: *Sink or Float Predictions and Conclusion (Kindergarten)*

Extension: *The teacher displayed the writing and added photographs, text, labels, and arrows to show the full investigation. (Note: They used* shared writing *to record their predictions and observations. The teacher wrote the students' ideas.)*

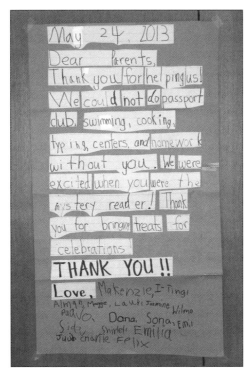

Interactive Writing Piece: *Thank-You Letter to Parents (Kindergarten)*

Extension: *The writing piece was hung on the classroom door so that parents could read it.*

Interactive Writing Piece: *Author Study of Eric Carle (Grade 1)*

Extensions: *(1) Students painted illustrations in the style of Eric Carle, and (2) the piece was displayed on a bulletin board.*

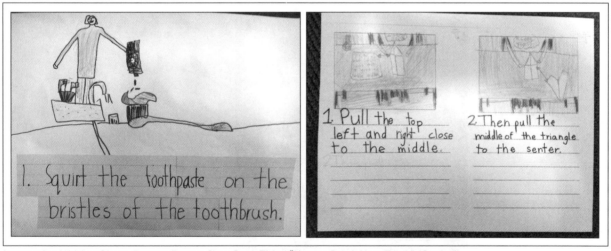

Interactive Writing Piece: *Excerpt From a Class Book Titled "How to Brush Your Teeth" (Grade 1)*

Extensions: *(1) The class-created piece was illustrated by the students and displayed on a classroom wall, and (2) students wrote their own how-to piece about a topic of their choice (e.g., How to Make a Paper Airplane).*

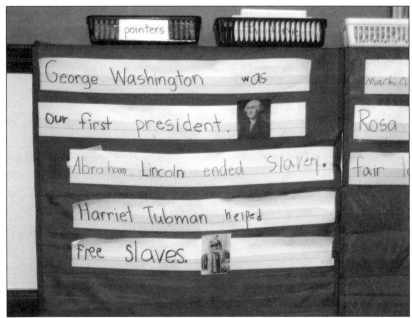

Interactive Writing Piece: *Informational Text About Historical Figures (Grade 1)*

Extension: *The text was placed in a pocket chart for students to read. (Notice the "pointers" above the chart for students to use when reading.)*

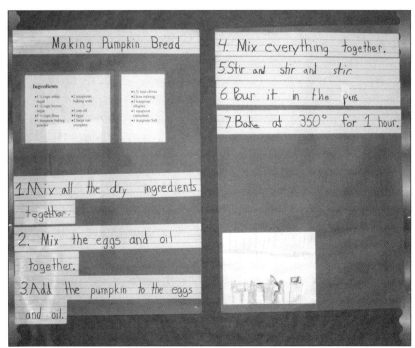

Interactive Writing Piece: *How to Make Pumpkin Bread (Grade 1)*

Extensions: *(1) The writing piece and a typed list of ingredients was displayed in the hallway near the classroom, and (2) the teacher photographed the bulletin board and sent home the recipe with each student.*

Holly was excited to go to the ball and meet a boy. Finally, the night had arrived. Holly was on her way, when suddenly a cage

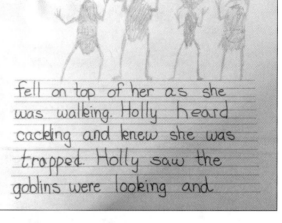

fell on top of her as she was walking. Holly heard cackling and knew she was trapped. Holly saw the goblins were looking and

laughing at her. She was scared because she was in the middle of the creepy, deep, dark woods and nobody could help her.

Once upon a time there lived a girl with a Blue cape. The people in her town said her cape shone so bright in the sunshine that they called her Little Blue Riding Hood. One day her mother said to her sweet daghter, go in the forest and pick some berries for your sick old grandfather. Little Blue Riding Hood understood and took a medium sized basket, said good-bye ①

and went in the forest. She found black berries, blue berries and rasberries. When she finished piking the berries, the old wolf, came up to her and said, "Let's have a nice party in my warm cozy cave." When she turned around she was surprised to see a wolf. She had never talked to a wolf. So she said, "Oh all right. I'll go with you." So she ②

Interactive Writing Piece: *Excerpt From a Fairy-Tale Adaptation Titled "Princess Holly" (Grade 2)*

Extensions: *(1) The teacher printed the fairy tale and gave a copy to each student to illustrate and bring home, and (2) each student adapted a different fairy tale (e.g., "Little Blue Riding Hood").*

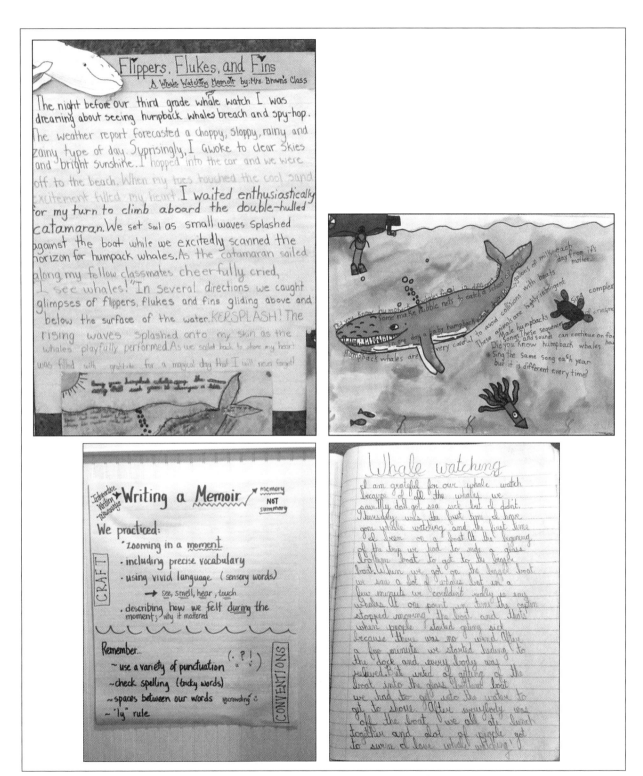

Interactive Writing Piece: *Memoir of a Whale-Watching Field Trip (on Chart Paper) (Grade 3)*

Extensions: *(1) Students painted images from their trip and incorporated fun facts about whales, (2) students wrote their own personal memoir of the trip, and (3) an anchor chart captured the key learning that took place during the memoir-writing lesson.*

The Supersonic Jaguar. ①

We are researching the jaguar. The jaguar is part of the Cat family.
It is big. It has black spots and golden fur underneath. It has sharp claws. It has pointy ears, a wet nose, and four strong legs. The jaguar lives all over South America except in Patagonia which is on the tip. The jaguar swims, runs and walks too.

Snakes have no legs and smell with their tongue.
The Boa looks like a long piece of thick string. The Boa Constrictor can be 6-19 feet long! The Boa Constrictor

③ slithers on the ground and some slither up trees. The Boa sees with its two eyes. The Boa has smooth dry scales. The Boa Constrictor stares at you.

Interactive Writing Piece: *Research on the Jaguar (Grade 3)*
Extension: *Students researched a second animal (e.g., boa constrictor) and included illustrations.*

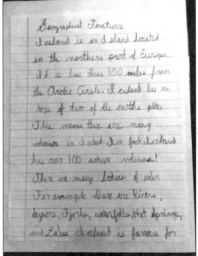

Interactive Writing Piece: *Research on Madagascar (Grade 3)*

Extensions: *(1) Students researched and wrote about another country (e.g., Iceland) using the same style and format, and (2) students created books about their country that were shared with parents during a celebration of world cultures.*

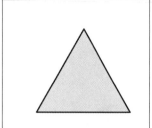
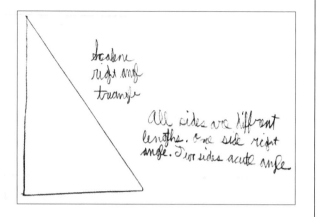

All sides are the same length. All angles are smaller than a right angle. They are acute angles.

scalene right angle triangle

All sides are different lengths. One side right angle. Two sides acute angle

Interactive Writing Piece: *Definition of an Equilateral Triangle (Grade 3)*

Extension: *Students sketched and defined other types of triangles.*

<Scene begins with Roxanne exploring a book about Magellan in her classroom.>

Roxanne (R): This is a great book about Magellan. Oooo, look there's a picture of Magellan on his ship! Let me take a closer look.

<Time machine sounds begin. Then you hear the sound of crashing waves. Roxanne is transported back in time. She appears on Magellan's ship.>

R: Where am I? Whoa! There's Ferdinand Magellan himself. I'm gonna go ask him some questions.

R: *<Roxanne pauses then yells out.>* Sir! Sir! Captain Magellan!

Magellan (M): *<Yelling back>* Who are you?!!! Why are you on my ship?!!

R: I'm Roxanne. I only wanted to ask you some questions.

M: And then you leave.

R: Yes Captain Magellan. When and where were you born?

M: I was born in Portugal in 1840. My parents died when I was 10.

R: Oh, I'm sorry. What happened to you then?

M: I was made to work as a page for a long time for Queen Leonor of Portugal. When I got older, I wanted to explore so I could find a way to reach the Spice Islands without having to sail around the Cape of Good Hope.

R: What motivated you to go on this journey?

M: I wanted to bring back spices to Portugal and become rich.

Interactive Writing Piece: *Script About an Explorer (Grade 4)*

Extensions: *(1) Students worked in pairs to write their own scripts about the explorer they researched, (2) they recorded their writing using GarageBand, and (3) recordings were shared with parents at an evening event.*

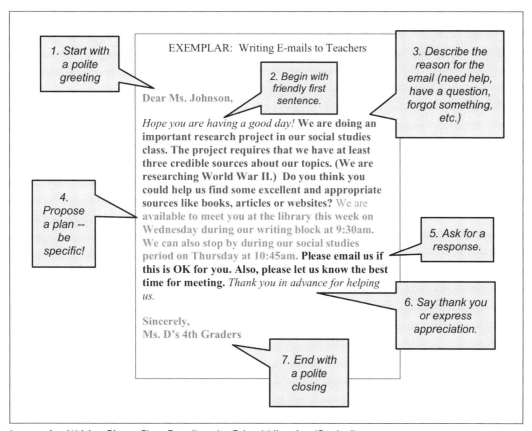

Interactive Writing Piece: *Class E-mail to the School Librarian (Grade 4)*

Extensions: *(1) The teacher sent the e-mail to the librarian, and (2) the teacher annotated the writing and turned it into a genre exemplar—Writing E-mails to Teachers*

How to Write a Letter to an Author

1. **Record** the date in the top left hand corner.
2. **Include** greeting
3. **Introduce** yourself
4. **Explain** why you are writing to him/her
5. **Thank** him/her for reading your letter
6. **Include** closing

How to Catch a Wave by Luke

1. Swim out past the impact zone to where the waves are about to crash.

2. Be Patient—don't just take the first one that comes!

When you see the wave you want . . .

3. Face the beach but turn your head to watch the approaching wave.

4. Kick your legs as fast as you can when the wave is coming close. (Fins can help you.)

5. Hold on to your board and let the wave take you to shore.

March 6, 2012

Dear Mr. _____,

Hi. My name is Jordan. I am in 4th grade. I live on the Big Island of Hawaii in _____. I have read your book, _____. While my classmates and I were reading your book we noticed an error. On page ___, paragraph two it says that Mauna Loa is the tallest volcano in the world. But, it is really the longest volcano on earth. You might want to change this error so that kids in the USA don't get the wrong information.

From,
Jordan

March 6, 2012

Dear Mr. _____,

My name is Riley and I'm in the 4th grade at the _____ school. I live in Hawaii on Mauna Kea. I read your book called _____ and I found an error on page ___ in the second paragraph. The error is that you said Mauna Loa is the tallest volcano. But seeing that I live on Mauna Kea, I know that Mauna Kea is taller than Mauna Loa. You should fix this mistake because people around the world who read your book will get the wrong information about Hawaii. Thank you for reading this Mr. _____.

Sincerely,
Riley

Interactive Writing Piece: *How to Write to an Author (Grade 4)*

Extensions: *(1) Students wrote their own how-tos (e.g., How to Catch a Wave), (2) the students used their interactive writing to guide them as they wrote letters to an author, and (3) the teacher sent the letters to the publishing company.*

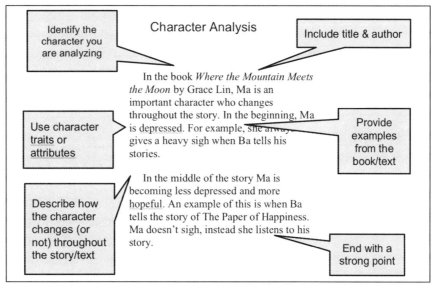

Character Analysis

Identify the character you are analyzing

Include title & author

In the book *Where the Mountain Meets the Moon* by Grace Lin, Ma is an important character who changes throughout the story. In the beginning, Ma is depressed. For example, she always gives a heavy sigh when Ba tells his stories.

Use character traits or attributes

Provide examples from the book/text

Describe how the character changes (or not) throughout the story/text

In the middle of the story Ma is becoming less depressed and more hopeful. An example of this is when Ba tells the story of The Paper of Happiness. Ma doesn't sigh, instead she listens to his story.

End with a strong point

Interactive Writing Piece: *Character Analysis (Grade 4)*

Extensions: *(1) The teacher used the piece as a genre exemplar, and (2) the students used the piece to guide them as they wrote their own character analysis.*

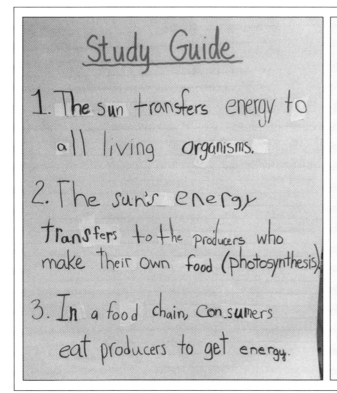

Study Guide

1. The sun transfers energy to all living organisms.

2. The sun's energy transfers to the producers who make their own food (photosynthesis).

3. In a food chain, Consumers eat producers to get energy.

Study Guide: Food Chains & Food Webs

Homework: Draw these ideas as you prepare for your test tomorrow!

1. The sun transfers energy to all living organisms.

2. The sun's energy transfers to the producers who make their own food (photosynthesis).

3. In a food chain, consumers eat producers to get energy.

Interactive Writing Piece: *Summary of Key Points From Unit on Living Things (Grade 5)*

Extension: *The key points became a study guide for students to use as they prepared for their test.*

Planning for Extend

As is always the case, the decision about how to extend a piece must be guided by your unique situation. Many times, you know the extension before you sit down with the class during Prewrite. For example, you knew you would mail the thank-you letter or use the piece as an exemplar of how to write a specific genre before students wrote their own. Sometimes the extension is obvious—you wrote a question for a graph that you need to complete or you are writing a book that you want students to reread, so you hang it on the wall as a "wall book."

Other times, the extension may emerge as you are writing the piece. In these instances, build off from the work completed during Prewrite, Compose, and Share the Pen. If you are writing a piece over the course of several days or a week, there may be short extensions you would like to do at the end of each lesson or later. Or new ideas for an extension may arise once the piece is complete. The suggestions in this chapter offer a range of ideas, but there may be other creative ways that make sense for the particular piece and for your students. Remember to match the extension with what will be most helpful for your writers and with what your curriculum requires of them.

Time is also a factor to consider as some extensions are longer than others. Sometimes a short extension serves a powerful purpose. For example, with primary students working on the concept of a word, a quick extension is to cut up the sentence word by word. Then you put the sentence back together. You could either put the words back together on the easel or have one student for each word hold a card and stand in front of the class as they move around to put the sentence in order. You might mix up the individual words and have the students put them in order in a pocket chart. (This eventually could be placed into a center for further extension.) This brief extension holds important value for emergent readers and writers, as it reinforces how each word is its own concept and how words are placed in a sequence from left to right to make a sentence.

A longer extension, such as students writing their own version of a piece or in another genre, is a worthwhile plan as well. In this situation, the extension may take several days or weeks as students practice and internalize the various craft elements or conventions with their own writing. As they move through the writing process, the interactive writing piece serves as the springboard, or a mentor text, to support their independent efforts. You can frequently remind students of the work they did as a class while they work on their individual pieces.

The decisions around type and length of an extension are yours to make. As you move through the school year, you want to balance longer extensions with shorter ones. You also want to mix up the types of extensions you do so that students learn about the many ways to celebrate and publish a piece. This keeps your interactive writing lessons fresh and exciting as you engage students creatively in this work.

Final Thoughts

During Extend, you and your students work with the completed interactive writing piece in a range of thoughtful and creative ways. There are many ways to extend a piece! Adding visuals, such as illustrations or photographs, creates an attractive product while supporting emergent readers who rely on visuals for meaning. Honoring the piece's real-world purpose by sharing it with its intended audience or using it in relevant classroom activities promotes the work that real authors do.

When you work through Extend, your students celebrate the writing in its published form and see themselves as capable authors. Revisiting the text itself is an extension that allows students to practice fluency and be reminded of important print concepts. Finished pieces can also be highlighted strategically to show students the key elements of a particular genre. Extensions can be short or long. Perhaps the most powerful part of Extend is when students take the skills and strategies learned in the interactive writing lesson and apply them directly to their own independent writing. Extend is where this happens.

Getting Started With Interactive Writing

CHAPTER 9

Eight Points for Preparation

Preparation and planning are the keys to a successful interactive writing lesson! Learn more about these important points for implementation and consider the following questions: What classroom management routines can help me prepare for a smooth interactive writing lesson? How should I organize my classroom and materials for a successful lesson? How do I plan thoughtfully for interactive writing?

Now that you have been introduced to interactive writing, it is time to give it a try in your classroom! In this chapter, we offer eight points to consider before you begin:

1. Teach routines first
2. Create a comfortable space for optimum learning
3. Highlight important writing resources
4. Use and organize materials in strategic ways
5. Prepare to make thoughtful teaching decisions
6. Consider carefully the time of day to deliver the lesson
7. Select the structure: whole class or small group
8. Be patient with yourself

Most of these points are not unique to interactive writing. They are the characteristics of good teaching in general. That said, interactive writing is a complex method of instruction that requires thoughtful planning. Intentional organization and solid classroom management will facilitate a smooth and productive experience for you and your class.

WHAT TEACHERS ARE SAYING

Don't give up on the first try! It takes practice to get the students used to the process, but if you stick with it, the rewards are plentiful. Prekindergarten is not too young to start interactive writing! I was a little skeptical at first. However, after the first lesson, I was blown away on how well my kids did and how much they enjoyed it.
—Krystle (PreK)

Ensuring Successful Implementation: Classroom Management 101

Interactive writing lessons are effective only when classroom management systems are solid. Our experience *as* teachers and *with* teachers reinforces that, in addition to knowing this method well and engaging in thoughtful lesson planning, attention must also be given to how your classroom flows and the expectations you have for students. With this in mind, we wander briefly into the world of classroom management in order to share some important conceptual understandings that undergird the practice of interactive writing. We also consider the work done by others who have written about interactive writing. Taken together, this thinking informs our points for preparation.

"An effective management system paves the way for learning to occur with minimal interference and maximal nourishment" (Saphier, Haley-Speca, & Gower, 2008, p. 17). Indeed, strong classroom management is a core foundation of effective teaching. Much has been studied, synthesized, and written about this topic. There are lists of tips and procedures available for teachers to use in a variety of moments (e.g., Lemov, 2014; Phelan & Schonour, 2004; Wong, Wong, Jondahl, & Ferguson, 2014). Others have researched and named key conceptual areas of classroom management and have noted their connection to child development and learning theories (e.g., Jones & Jones, 2013; Marzano, Marzano, & Pickering, 2003).

Several authors have written specifically about interactive writing. Some offer lists of materials and classroom routines to help with an efficient lesson (Callella & Jordano, 2000; McCarrier et al., 2000; Swartz, Klein, & Shook, 2001). Others have proposed grouping options to promote student success (Tompkins & Collom, 2004). McCarrier et al. (2000) offer detailed guidance for K–2 teachers about how to organize space and plan for lessons. There are also self-assessment rubrics for you to evaluate your instruction during an interactive writing lesson (McCarrier et al., 2000; Swartz et al., 2001).

Key Areas to Keep in Mind for Interactive Writing

In his comprehensive text *The Skillful Teacher*, Saphier and his colleagues identify six essential areas of classroom management: attention, momentum, space, time, routines, and discipline (Saphier et al., 2008). Five of these areas— attention, momentum, space, time, and routines—are especially helpful as you begin interactive writing. (Our thinking is that if these areas of management are well attended to, then discipline challenges will decrease.)

- *Attention* is about how you engage students, how you initiate your lesson, and how you keep students focused. Gaining attention works well when you respond to what students are showing you. For example, if they are highly energized, you may need to use a calming voice. Or if they appear lethargic or withdrawn, then it is time to motivate them through an energetic approach. Attention is also achieved when you show enthusiasm for the lesson and have a sense of humor. Enjoying the lesson yourself is a powerful way to maintain student interest. Incorporating physical movement into a lesson can activate the brain in powerful ways.

- *Momentum* has to do with keeping the lesson flow paced appropriately. It requires you to have materials ready to go and be mindful of how to move the lesson forward with the least number of interruptions. A particularly salient quality of momentum is anticipation: the forward-thinking ability that allows you to know and plan for any possible lesson derailment. Skillful teachers anticipate the vulnerable points in their lessons and have a plan in mind to address them—before the lesson begins.

- *Space* involves how you arrange the furniture, equipment, and materials thoughtfully in order to maximize instruction. Saphier et al. (2008) write that space should match instruction. For example, if student collaboration is needed as part of a lesson, then the space should support this by ensuring students can talk and work with their peers easily.

- *Time* considers how teachers "manage student time for maximum learning" (Saphier et al., 2008, p. 49). Interestingly, Saphier and his colleagues identify *interactive* instruction as the most important use of time for students. This form of instruction includes moments of direct teaching combined with student input and processing opportunities for students. Moreover, Saphier et al. assert that during interactive instruction "students are actively engaged in all phases of the learning experience" (p. 56).

- *Routines* encompass the many repetitive activities that occur in classrooms every day. There are routines around logistics (e.g., taking attendance, collecting lunch money, lining up), routines around work time (e.g., how to work with a partner, what noise level is acceptable), and routines during instructional moments (e.g., how to respond to a question, how to sit and be ready to listen, how to turn and talk with a peer). Without solid routines in place, you lose valuable time redirecting students or responding to confusion. Saphier et al. (2008) recommend that routines are as follows:

o Articulated clearly, repeated, and practiced until students have mastered them

o Modeled for students

o Articulated in a positive way (e.g., "We will work hard to…" or "We are successful when we…")

o "Tenaciously adhered to until integrated" (p. 69)

Table 18 shows how these essential areas of management can be applied to interactive writing. As you begin your implementation, you will want to think through these ideas and be proactive about how you plan to address them. To support you, we discuss these connections in greater depth in our eight points of preparation.

Getting Started With Interactive Writing: Eight Points of Preparation

Building off the ideas described earlier, the eight points that follow represent our best thinking and the thinking of many teachers with whom we have worked on how to begin using interactive writing. Taken together, they can cue important planning work and support your early efforts with the method.

1. Teach Routines First

Familiarity with routines and procedures will free your students from distractions and encourage them to focus on the important learning about the craft and conventions of writing. *You* will also benefit because you will be able to focus more on the teaching decisions as the flow of the lesson becomes effortless.

Take time in the first few weeks of lessons to break down procedures to the smallest detail, such as how students need to move up to the easel or computer quickly when it is their turn to write or how to stand off to the side when using a pointer to lead the class in rereading so that all students can see the text.

For example, we have seen teachers of young students put a dot on the floor so the students know where to stand. You should teach and have students practice the way you want them to sit during a lesson and how to engage (e.g., use the name chart, reread in unison, turn and talk with a partner, share an idea, write "in the air"). All of this should be done in a positive and upbeat

Table 18 Classroom Management and Interactive Writing

Management Area	How It Applies to Interactive Writing
Attention	*Think about how you will...* • Begin the lesson and keep students engaged throughout each phase (Prewrite, Compose, Share the Pen, and Review) • Support their high/low energy by adjusting your teaching voice and actions to keep them "with you" • Show enthusiasm for the work they are doing during all phases of the lesson • Bring humor and joy to the lesson
Momentum	*Anticipate...* • The different materials you will need for the lesson • The parts of the lesson that may be challenging (Compose, Share the Pen) and your plan for guiding students through that challenge • The pacing of the lesson (e.g., where will you need to slow down so that students can build off each other, when/how will you finalize the wording of the sentence during Compose in order to move the lesson along) • Whom you will select to share ideas during Compose or who will write during Share the Pen/Keyboard • How you will keep the whole class engaged during Share the Pen/Keyboard (e.g., what techniques will you use while one student is writing/typing) • The sensitivity a student may feel if selected (or not selected) to participate during a particular phase of the lesson (e.g. Compose, Share the Pen/Keyboard)
Space	*Plan for...* • A well-organized location that allows all students to be engaged in the lesson through collaborative interactions • Where and how students will sit (e.g. on the rug, chairs) • An optimum location for materials, especially the easel, or screen • A special location near you for a student who may be more/less sensitive to peers (e.g., calls out often, shy or withdrawn, struggles to sit in a calm way)
Time	*Schedule interactive writing...* • When you and the students can bring your best energy and focus (e.g., first part of the day, directly after lunch or recess) • Regularly so that students become familiar with the lesson sequence
Routines	*Determine...* • The routines you need/want in place for a successful lesson (e.g., where to sit, how to share ideas during Compose, how to reread the writing) • How you will introduce and practice the routines • If a new routine is needed or if an existing routine is not working; have a plan for revisiting routines throughout the year

Note. Based on *The Skillful Teacher: Building Your Teaching Skills* (6th ed.), by J. Saphier, M. Haley-Speca, and R. Gower, 2008, Acton, MA: Research for Better Teaching.

rather than punitive way. *Teach* these routines and your expectations clearly and explicitly. Model and *practice* (and practice and practice again!) each element of the lesson.

We also recommend that early on you offer all students the opportunity to write or type (e.g., use equity sticks, have a running list of who has participated so far). Moving forward, not every student will be called to participate in every lesson. However, each student needs to practice the routine of being the scribe so he or she knows how to do this efficiently when selected in future lessons. You should explain to the class that not everyone holds the pen (or types on the keyboard) every time, but that over the course of the weeks and months everyone will have many chances to type and write.

Talking as a class community about how to manage the feelings and emotions that sometimes arise when you are not called on or when your ideas are not fully included may be important. Students can learn and practice routines around how to be patient, listen to a friend's ideas, or wait until it is their turn. Being proactive about this not only supports a smoother lesson but also fosters resiliency and self-regulation as students take responsibility for their social-emotional development. Emphasize that *every* student is participating as a *group* member in *every* lesson. Table 19 captures a range of the important routines you may need to teach students as you take on this method.

Table 19 Possible Routines for Interactive Writing

Movement	*How do we…* • Transition into/out of interactive writing (e.g., come to the rug, move into "up close" seating)? • Move up to the easel or screen? • Lead the class to reread what is written (e.g., use the pointer, track the print)?
Discussion	*How do we…* • Share our ideas about the topic? • Listen to what others say? • Wait for our turn to talk? • Build our ideas off one another? • Accept the final decision about a sentence? • Support our peers with ideas and suggestions in positive/helpful ways?
Scribing (Writing or Typing)	*How do we…* • Use the pen to write? • Type on the keyboard? • Use whiteboards and markers to practice a writing convention? • Fix our errors when they occur (e.g., correction tape, spell-check, grammar check)? • Stay focused and engaged while one student is writing or typing?
Extension	*How do we…* • Display our writing (where does it go?)? • Share our writing with others? • Apply the writing principles taught to our independent writing?

The ultimate goal, of course, is to keep your students engaged in the writing process to maximize the potential of the lesson. We cannot emphasize enough that it is a worthy investment of your time to tenaciously *teach* your students the many routines that will make interactive writing a seamless experience for all. The more you invest in this work early on, the more productive and joyful the lessons will be.

2. Create a Comfortable Space for Optimum Learning

Because interactive writing is a community experience, proximity to one another and to the place of writing matters. The shared nature of the task requires bringing everyone together in a supportive arrangement. It is also essential that everyone is comfortable and can easily see the easel or screen and any other helpful writing resources you plan to use (e.g., name chart, graphic organizer). As you perhaps have noticed throughout the book, in the primary grades, students should be seated on a large rug as you facilitate the lesson from a chair or stool up front. This arrangement works well for older students too. (Yes, fourth and fifth graders can sit on the rug!)

Students Gather on the Rug for Interactive Writing (PreK)

That said, we recognize that there are other ways to ensure a comfortable space. Having older students sit "up close" in chairs can work well. There may also be times in upper-grade classrooms where the interactive writing lesson is effective when students are seated at their desks for turn-and-talks or quick table conversations. Keep in mind, the arrangement and seating decisions you make matter. Proximity *is* important. If students are seated too far away, it is likely that their ability to focus may be compromised. The guiding principle is to ensure that students can see the easel or screen clearly, can participate with ease, and can stay engaged in the lesson.

Students Sitting "Up Close" in Chairs (Grade 4)

Students Discuss at Their Desks During Compose (Grade 5)

3. Highlight Important Writing Resources

The ultimate goal of interactive writing lessons is to foster students' independence as writers. Therefore, throughout the lesson your students should practice using classroom resources that they can and should use during their own writing. For example, during the lesson, you may refer to the name chart, alphabet chart, or word wall. In upper-grade classrooms, having anchor charts to guide students or to create vocabulary word banks that align with the lesson might be helpful. In some classes, teachers regularly use a thesaurus (either a hard copy or an online version). Highlighting these tools during the interactive writing lesson shows students how they help writers and models your expectation that students should use these resources when they write independently.

4. Use and Organize Materials in Strategic Ways

Teachers have found that some types of materials (e.g., paper, pens, markers) can distract from the potential learning opportunities of an interactive writing lesson. For example, chart paper without lines can be problematic because students have difficulty focusing on handwriting without clear lines to guide them. In addition, multicolored messages are often hard to read and marker choice can become a distraction. Young students do best with sentence strips with handwriting lines.

For upper-elementary-grade students, teach them to use two lines for print, with the middle line indicating the midway point for "tall" versus "short" letters. This uniformity helps in the readability of the message. In addition to the ruled paper, a sharp black marker is the clearest writing tool because the color is bold and uniform. For a more colorful presentation, mount the strips or chart on colorful paper and encourage students to illustrate the writing during Extend.

Word Wall (Grade 2)

In Chapter 6, we identified important materials needed for this method (See Table 14 on page 109). Having these materials well organized so that no time is lost during the lesson searching for a black marker that works or running back to your desk to grab the correcting tape is important. Have your materials ready!

For example, fastening a marker to the easel ensures that one will always be available. You might have a special spot (e.g., a small basket or bin nearby) where you keep your correcting tape, sticky notes, a pen, and your lesson plan. Some teachers keep their list of "kids to call on" handy so that they do not forget in the moment. Other teachers have come up with creative ways to manage the marker boards and erasers that they use during the lesson. As you get started, develop a system that works for you and your students. This way, the lesson will flow and materials will be incorporated effortlessly.

An Easel Prepared and Ready for Interactive Writing (Grade 1)

5. Prepare to Make Thoughtful Teaching Decisions

As discussed throughout this book, the most effective interactive writing lessons are those that are well planned. This means reading and analyzing your students' writing routinely. Some teachers find it helpful to record these anecdotal observations onto a one-page document that informs their lessons (see Figure 3). Notice these notes are informal yet provide critical insights about what your students are doing well and what support they need from you. You may opt to build and update these weekly or monthly depending upon your grade level.

At the same time, you must keep in mind the overarching writing expectations required by your district or school curriculum and any specific writing genre unit you may be implementing. Interactive writing is a teaching approach that can advance both the individualized needs of writers and any grade-level goals simultaneously. With thoughtful advanced planning, your teaching decisions will be strategic and most effective.

Figure 3 Sample Notes on Student Writing (Grade 2)

Student	Doing Well With...	Needs Support With...
Alicia	High-frequency words; spelling	Organizing her thoughts; handwriting
Alex	Lots of good ideas in his pieces; his depth and details are precise	Ready for more complex sentences and vocabulary (above grade level)
Ashley	Handwriting	Push for more complex sentences
Braden	Starts out strong; runs out of momentum when he writes	How to end a piece; complete a project
Christian	Great voice in his writing; clever phrases	Conventions—handwriting; following capitalization rules
Cooper	Draws pictures and sketches	All areas; needs to see himself as a writer
Dante	Creative/interesting ideas	Stretching his ideas, handwriting, punctuation, spacing
Darlene	Conventions—presentation	Word choice—push her to move beyond simple "safe" words (Frend/friend)
Denise	Enjoys writing, lots of ideas	General support in all areas; organization
Evan	Detailed drawings and simple sentences	Sentence fluency; stretching his words into complete sentences
Ignacio	Conventions, handwriting; sketches	Word choice; vocabulary; grammar rules
Jessie	Voice; word choice	Spelling and punctuation (their/there)
Kylen	Organization; motivated to write	Word choice; taking a risk with more complex vocab words ("like" "fun" "love")
Michael	Fluency; motivated to write	Organization; saying his ideas precisely and avoiding repetition
Rachel	Handwriting, spelling, organization	Voice and sentence fluency; moving beyond simple sentences
Stacey	Fluency; motivated to write	Organizing ideas; spelling (becus, shun/tion)
Shawn	Voice; creative phrases; vocabulary	Organization of ideas; staying on topic; spelling
Terese	Handwriting, layout/spacing, drawings	Connecting ideas with words; moving from words to phrases
Victoria	Simple ideas; specific tasks	Seeing herself as a writer, moving her talk into written text; spelling of HFW

There are multiple ways you might plan for interactive writing. Some teachers find it best to plan for each individual interactive writing lesson (see Figure 4). Alternatively, you might plan for multiple days of an interactive writing project (see Figure 5). In both versions, notice that each phase of the lesson is identified and that many of the teaching decisions have been made in advance around what will be written and how the writing will be extended. Also notice that the plans identify the craft and conventions you will address

Figure 4 Sample Planning Sheet for Each Session of Interactive Writing (Grade 4)

Date/Duration: *October (1 day lesson; 30 minutes)*
Subject: *ELA*

Experience	**What are we writing about today?** *Continued work on book review of Bud, Not Buddy*
Prewrite	**Purpose:** *Strengthen how we end our writing; satisfy readers and leave them thinking more* **Audience:** *Students will use the final piece as an exemplar for their own writing* **Genre:** *Book review*
Compose	**Craft Priorities (organization, ideas, word choice, sentence fluency, voice):** *organization—emphasize the qualities of a strong/satisfying/interesting ending* *ideas—what are 2–3 "big ideas" we want to highlight from Bud, Not Buddy* *word choice—choose precise words that provide specific details from the text* *voice—show our enthusiasm about the book* *sentence fluency – push for more complex/interesting sentence* **Students to Select:** *Darius or Tiffany (organization); Kevin (word choice or voice); Lyneka (sentence fluency)*
Share the Pen (Keyboard)	**Important Conventions to Include (spelling, grammar, handwriting, punctuation, etc.):** *grammar—verb tense (future vs. conditional tense)* *spelling—multisyllabic words!!* *keyboarding—practice commas, spacing, and capitalization* **Students to Select:** *Calvin and Mariko (keyboarding); Damon (grammar); Tamara (spelling)*
Review	**Three Points to Review:** ***qualities of strong ending* *grammar: tense* *spelling: whatever words come up*
Extend	**What will we do with the piece? (e.g., exemplar, send/give to author, display, add visuals)** *Students will use this as an exemplar as they write their own book reviews.*

Figure 5 Sample Planning Sheet for Multiple Days of Interactive Writing (Grade 1)

Date/Duration: *February; should take about two weeks to write the book; one sentence or page written per day for approximately 15 minutes*

Subject: *ELA*

Experience	**What are we writing about today?** *our own retelling of "The Three Pigs"*
Prewrite	**Purpose:** *synthesize different versions we have read to write our own* **Audience:** *everyone who walks by to read our wall book* **Genre:** *folktale*
Compose	**Craft Priorities (organization, ideas, word choice, sentence fluency, voice):** *organization—beginning, middle, end* *voice—use language from our favorite versions (James Marshall!)* **Students to Select:** *Alex (staying on topic), Lauren (combining ideas), Matt B, Josh (sequence / what comes next?)*
Share the Pen (Keyboard)	**Important Conventions to Include (spelling, grammar, handwriting, punctuation, etc.):** *spelling—word wall ("snap words"), multisyllabic words, beginning blends* *Capitals at beginning, periods at end of sentence. Mostly lowercase.* *Tall letters and short letters* **Students to Select:** *Sade (space between words), Kim, David, Lauren (snap words), Vennetia, Matty (multisyllable), Bryce (blends), Gregory, Adam (end punctuation)*
Review	**Three Points to Review:** *snap word, blend sound, period or quotation mark—depends on teaching points!!*
Extend	**What will we do with the piece? (e.g., exemplar, send/give to author, display, add visuals)** *Illustrate (small groups for collages), display as wall book* *Board book to hang in hall outside class. Students will work in pairs to make collage illustrations.*

and list the specific students to involve at particular moments during the lesson. This intentional piece of planning speaks to the differentiation that you want to prepare for ahead of the lesson. Knowing which students need support and specifically the kind of support needed is imperative as you plan. Doing this thinking before the lesson allows you to thoughtfully select students during Compose and Share the Pen.

If you plan for an overall project, you likely will revisit and refine your plan after each individual lesson and as the project develops. This is the organic nature of the method. Depending on how much is written and how the writing evolves, you can adjust the next lesson accordingly. You can use the lesson plan template in Figure 6 to help with your planning.

Finally, as you look at these sample plans, recognize that there are moments that *cannot* be planned in advance. The organic nature of the method requires you to expect the unexpected and to embrace this. Perhaps the best way to name this is to "plan for the unplanned." When you work through the Review phase of the lesson, you will highlight the two or three planned (or unplanned) teaching moments that are most relevant for your students.

6. Consider Carefully the Time of Day to Deliver the Lesson

Another important point to consider is the time of day when interactive writing takes place. As mentioned before, time devoted for this important interactive instruction is time well spent. Moreover, as we have described in this book, interactive writing demands a high level of focus from students. It is therefore essential that the students come to each lesson ready and able to be attentive.

As we talked about in Chapter 2, we recommend short, daily lessons in grades PreK–1. As you move up in the grades, the frequency and duration of the lessons will change on the basis of the needs of your writers. How you fit it in each day or week can be flexible to meet your unique scheduling needs. That said, there are few important factors to keep in mind.

First, in the primary grades, because the lessons are brief (10–15 minutes), there are many creative ways to fit this method into your busy day. For example, you might start each day with a lesson or fit it in right after recess or lunch. The logic here is that students will be coming "fresh" to the lesson from unique activities outside of the classroom. This scheduling tip works for grades 2–5 as well.

Alternatively in the primary grades, you might have small blocks of time open in your day where you can squeeze in interactive writing. For example, if music ends 20 minutes before lunch begins, interactive writing can fit nicely there. If, however, interactive writing is scheduled back to back with another academic subject, providing some type of transition time (e.g., quick stretch break, some quick physical movement) or switching the seating arrangement (e.g., move students from tables to the rug or from their desks into "up close" seating) to help students focus on the lesson is recommended. The goal here is to prime students for a successful lesson and to avoid long stretches of time seated in the same location.

Finally, having it occur at predictable times each day and week can help students anticipate and get their minds ready for it. We recognize that scheduling

WHAT TEACHERS ARE SAYING

Don't give up if it doesn't work out the way you want it to the first few times. Like anything worthwhile, lessons become more natural and get better with practice. The only way to improve is to keep trying to find out what works for you.

—Heather (Kindergarten)

Figure 6 Lesson Plan Template for Interactive Writing

Date/Duration:

Subject:

Experience	What are we writing about today?
Prewrite	Purpose: Audience: Genre:
Compose	Craft Priorities (organization, ideas, word choice, sentence fluency, voice): Students to Select:
Share the Pen (Keyboard)	Important Conventions to Include (spelling, grammar, handwriting, punctuation, etc.): Students to Select:
Review	Three Points to Review:
Extend	What will we do with the piece? (e.g., exemplar, send/give to author, display, add visuals)

is a complex task: Our guidance here is to be as thoughtful as possible about when interactive writing happens in order to ensure the optimum experience for you and your students.

7. Select the Structure: Whole Class or Small Group

Interactive Writing in a Whole-Class Setting. Interactive writing works very well as a whole-class lesson.

In fact, all of the steps, routines, and practical advice shared throughout this book were designed for whole-class implementation. It is a unique method of teaching, in that it offers individualized instruction within a whole-class lesson. As we talked about in Compose, Share the Pen, and Review, you are able and encouraged to teach a range of skills and strategies throughout the lesson, and it therefore appeals to a large, heterogeneous group.

Another strength of including your entire class is that, when all of your students are contributing their ideas about a shared topic, there are more voices and more diverse ideas put forth. This can create robust conversations throughout each step in the lesson.

Perhaps the most compelling reason, however, for using this method for whole-class instruction is its potential to create a classroom community. As you fill your classroom with interactive writing pieces about shared experiences, you tell the "story of your class." In some ways the collection of writing is like a family photo album, illustrating the experiences and journey you have all shared *together*. Further, as you extend the pieces to become educational resources with ongoing value beyond the specific lesson, the idea that they were created by *all* means they can be used by *all* in the most meaningful ways.

Interactive Writing in a Small-Group Setting. There will be moments across your teaching day when a small-group writing lesson is the most appropriate structure for your students. Interactive writing works well here too. The lesson sequence remains the same, but there are important differences to highlight. First, in both whole-class and small-group structures, a *shared* experience remains essential. When working with a small group, you might opt to use a shared, *whole-class* experience in different ways. For example, one group of students might summarize the field trip to the farm, while another group writes a thank-you letter to the farmer who gave the tour, while a third group writes a factual piece about how farms work. Alternatively, in a small-group setting, it may be that the experience is shared only by the *group* of

WHAT TEACHERS ARE SAYING

Jump into it. It gets easier by the minute and after a few days you will ask yourself how you were able to teach writing at all before coming across interactive writing.

—Cristina (Kindergarten)

students with whom you are working. For example, a literature discussion group might engage in an interactive writing piece based on the book they are reading.

Second, the extensions for small-group interactive writing hold value only for those students who participated in the lesson. Consider again the farm field trip example. If students practiced how to write facts about the farm versus opinions about farms when they wrote their piece, they may be primed to practice this same skill in their own writing. It would not make sense for the whole class to take this on because it was a small-group teaching point. Thus, only these students use the piece as an exemplar. Small-group interactive writing can be displayed in your classroom. However, keep in mind that the whole-class community has not authored these pieces, so the influence of the writing will be limited. It may be that other extensions are more beneficial.

The strengths of small-group interactive writing are both the differentiation it allows and the intimacy it promotes. Pulling together a small group of students who may need specific support in writing allows you to focus and target your instruction in a meaningful way. And a group of six to eight students guided by a teacher will likely have more opportunities to talk during Compose and write during Share the Pen.

When making the decision of whether to teach a whole-class interactive writing lesson or a small-group interactive writing lesson, ask yourself the following planning questions:

- Who will benefit from this teaching? All students? A small group of students?

- What is the purpose of this lesson? What writing strategies around craft and conventions do I need to teach these writers?

- What experience will inform the writing? A whole-class experience or a small-group experience?

- What extension will best support these writers?

8. Be Patient With Yourself

Last but not least, we consider a point for preparation that centers on *you*, the teacher! Finding a natural rhythm in interactive writing takes time. To help, we recommend that you use the method frequently as you begin your school year. Your students will learn quickly and remember the predictable steps of interactive writing—especially if they participate in daily lessons (in grades PreK–2) or weekly lessons (in grades 3–5) early on in the year.

This repeated experience may also prompt you to make adjustments around space, materials, and organization. You might even find that you need to rethink when you have scheduled it. All of these adjustments are a natural part of the adult learning process. Planning, pacing, and management are often considered and reconsidered as teachers and students become more comfortable. As classroom routines become more secure, you will be able to hone your instruction, refining it to better meet the needs of your students.

As with any new learning, there may be bumps along the way. The best planned lesson may not go as you hope, or classroom management issues may seem secure one day and fall apart the next. Your routines and systems might not work each and every time. Sometimes the collaborative conversations during Compose may seem unwieldy or hard to wrap up. The writing during Share the Pen might not turn out how you had envisioned.

We have experienced and observed all of these implementation growing pains. We urge you to overcome these issues by working with a colleague or coach who can observe your lessons and give you helpful feedback. Or take time on your own to reflect on your teaching using your plans, detailed notes, or self-assessment rubrics (McCarrier et al., 2000; Swartz et al., 2001). Consider what is working well and where to make adjustments. For example, if student behavior seems problematic during Compose, consider more structures for how students are arranged and how they participate. If Compose conversations seem to stray, tighten your facilitation of the conversation and keep bringing students back to the craft element you know they need to practice. Said another way: Release responsibility when students are ready for it—but pull back and support them more if they are showing you they need help. In time, the challenges will diminish. Be patient with yourself and stay committed to the method!

Final Thoughts

As you prepare for interactive writing, take time to consider the important elements of classroom management. Specifically, think about the routines you and your students will need to have in place. Think also about your space and organization of materials. Schedule the lessons at optimum times and take advantage of using interactive writing in both whole-class and small-group lessons. Remember, interactive writing is a structured—*not scripted*—approach to writing instruction. There are creative ways that can make this method your own. It may be in how you cue students to share their ideas or the systems you put in place for how to organize materials. You might have unique places where you can display the written pieces. We hear from so many teachers that this is something they truly appreciate about interactive writing: There are *many* ways to do it well! Embrace this by matching the practice to your style of teaching.

CHAPTER 10

Pulling It All Together

Revisit interactive writing one last time by seeing how the lesson progresses from beginning to end! This cohesive and comprehensive approach is strengthened by five overarching principles that run through all grade levels. Consider these guiding questions: How do the multiple steps within interactive writing come together? What key principles should we keep in mind when using this method?

By now, you can see that interactive writing is an organized and structured approach to instruction, with each lesson following a predictable sequence. To help you understand the details and nuances of the method well, we zoomed in on each step in isolation, as if under a microscope. In reality, a lesson is quite fluid. For example, Prewrite flows easily into Compose, and Review naturally grows out of Compose and Share the Pen. In this chapter, we feature a complete lesson from each grade to show how all the pieces of the practice are pulled together to form a cohesive and comprehensive lesson.

This chapter concludes with five universal principles for interactive writing for grades PreK–5. As noted in Chapter 9, we encourage you to bring your own teaching style to this method. You should also make adjustments to your teaching as writers mature. That said, there are core ideas that hold for every interactive writing lesson across all grades.

A Picture Is Worth a Thousand Words: Part Two

In Chapter 1, we shared finished interactive writing pieces with you in order to introduce the method. Completed pieces are a window into the process in which the class engaged. We end in the same style, using a finished piece representing each grade to highlight how a lesson comes together. Throughout most of this book, we focused on pieces one step at a time—just looking at how they were composed or just looking at conventions featured during Share the Pen. Now is the time to see how all the steps in interactive writing come together to form a cohesive and comprehensive instructional approach for your students. In these one-page summaries, we highlight what teachers focused on at every stage of the process.

Experience
The class was engaged in a science unit on the five senses.

Prewrite
They planned to write a sentence on each sense. The teacher explained that they would make posters to share what they learned with others who visited their classroom.

Compose
They reread the two posters from the senses already completed. Then they discussed what they do with their nose and formed one concise sentence beginning with the word *we*.

Share the Pen
They focused on:
• Spaces between words
• Capital letter at the beginning of a sentence
• Letter formation
• High-frequency word *we*
• Listening to the first sound or two sounds at the beginning of a word
• Putting a period at the end of a sentence
Notice that the teacher chose to write the *ell* in *smell*, the *ith* in *with*, and the *ou* in *our*.

Review
Find...
• The word *we*
• The first word in our sentence
• The mark that tells us to stop reading
• A tall letter that goes to the top of the line

Extend
• The teacher cut the sentence into individual words and reassembled it on the easel as the last activity in the lesson. The students counted the number of words written that day.
• Each sentence was mounted on a poster to hang on the wall for rereading. The posters were illustrated with photos of the students pointing to the described body part.

Frequency and Duration
The class worked on their posters for five consecutive days. Each day they wrote about one sense in a lesson lasting approximately 10–15 minutes.

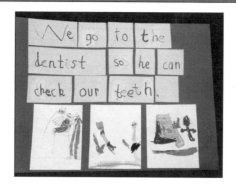

Experience
The class was engaged in a social studies unit on making healthy choices.

Prewrite
The teacher said they would write a book to teach others in the school about good health.

Compose
Each day they discussed healthy choices and decided which one to write about. This sentence involved combining two ideas: "We go to the dentist." *and* "He checks our teeth."

Share the Pen
They focused on:
• Spaces between words
• Spelling high-frequency "snap words": *We*, *go*, *to*, *the*, *so*, *he*, *can*
• Handwriting and letter formation
• Period at the end of the sentence
• Uppercase at the beginning of a sentence and lowercase for other letters
• Saying words slowly and listening to sounds in words (*dentist*, *check*, *teeth*)
• /Ch/ (*check*) and /th/ (*teeth*)
Notice that the teacher wrote the *ou* in *our*.

Review
Find...
• The capital letter (and tell why it is uppercase)
• The snap word *the*
• The period
Count...
• How many sentences we wrote

Extend
• The teacher cut the sentence into individual words and gave each word to a student. The students rearranged themselves in front of the class to put the sentence back together while the students who were sitting read to make sure it was correct.
• Each page of the book was mounted on large paper and illustrated by the students, with a few students contributing to each page.

Frequency and Duration
The class worked on their book about good health every day for eight days. Each day they wrote about one healthy choice in a lesson lasting between 15 and 20 minutes.

Experience
The class was engaged in a science unit on the four seasons.

Prewrite
The teacher said they would write a description about each of the seasons to share with the school community.

Compose
Each day they began by rereading what they had already written. Next, they discussed the season about which they would write. There was much emphasis on describing the season in a way that *everyone* could relate to rather than writing about an experience unique to one student. For example, when one student shared that she visited her aunt in another state every summer, they talked about the more general voice for this piece. Combining multiple ideas into one sentence was practiced (e.g., "We can go to the beach, the pool, and amusement parks, too.") The phrase "amusement parks" was suggested after several students named specific fun parks they visited. The students reread the piece often to listen to the sound of the sentences together and to ensure there was sentence variation in length and flow rather than having each sentence begin in the same way and follow a similar structure.

(continued)

Share the Pen

They focused on:

• High-frequency "snap words:" *it, in, the, and, are, of, we, can, get, to*
• *To* versus *too*
• Blends: *fl* (*flowers*), *pl* (*plants*)
• Uppercase letters at beginning of sentence and for months
• *-er* in *summer* and *longer* like *Jennifer* and *Christopher*
• *S* at end of word for plural: *flowers, plants, parks*
• Spelling words with multiple syllables: *vacation* and *amusement*
• Handwriting: "tall," "short," and "below the line" letters
• Period at end of sentence

Review

Find…

• A word where we added an *s* to make something more than one
• A word with more than two syllables
• The two ways we wrote *to* and *too* and tell us why
• The snap word (it, in, the, and, are , of, we, can , get, too)
• A word that ends like Jennifer and Christopher

Count…

• How many sentences we wrote

Extend

Each poster was decorated in a collage style. The students drew pictures to represent the season and cut out photos from a magazine. The four posters were hung together in the classroom, and the students used them for reading around the room and writing around the room activities.

Frequency and Duration

This page took four days to write, as the students composed and wrote one or two sentences a day. The students participated in interactive writing every day for approximately 15–20 minutes.

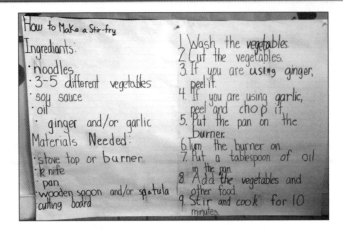

Experience
As part of a unit on China, the students cooked a stir-fry in class.

Prewrite
The teacher decided they would write the recipe so they could remember what they did and could enjoy making it again at home.

Compose
Features of a how-to (specifically a recipe) were emphasized, including writing a list of ingredients and materials needed, numbering steps, starting each direction with an action verb, and recording each step sequentially and with enough detail so the recipe could be followed easily.

Share the Pen
They focused on:
• Lowercase letters for items in the list; uppercase letters for the first letter of the first word in each step
• Strategies for spelling multisyllable words (e.g., *vegetables*, *ingredients*, *spatula*)
• /er/ sound: *er*, *ir*, *ur* (e.g., *ginger*, *stir*, *burner*)
• Using a comma to pause
• Layout: using number, bullets, list format

Review
Find...
• A place we used a comma and tell us why
• A word with four syllables and explain the strategy we used to spell this word
Explain...
• The important features of writing a recipe.

Extend
The teacher photographed the recipe and made copies to send home with each student.

Frequency and Duration
This piece took three days to write. The title and ingredient list was completed on the first day. The recipe steps were written over the following two days. The lessons lasted approximately 20 minutes.

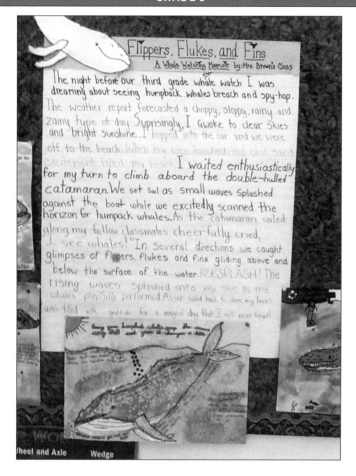

Experience
The students went on a whale-watching trip as part of their study of the ocean.

Prewrite
The school's third-grade ELA curriculum included writing memoirs. To begin, the teacher highlighted several genre features of memoirs (e.g., a memory told from one specific point of view, based on the truth, reveals the writer's feelings, focused on the experience rather than only on the event). The students then planned their memoir through journaling and brainstorming on their own. They focused in on only the most important points and details of their trip so that they could remember it and could post it for others in the school community to read.

Compose
The teacher worked intentionally on having a strong beginning and ending that captured their feelings, identifying the important moments of the trip, and using vivid language. Sentence fluency also was emphasized, as students were encouraged to build complex sentences using strong verbs and adverbs. Dialogue was included along with sound effects in order to bring their authentic voice into the memoir.

(continued)

Share the Pen

They focused on:

• The spelling of unique words and technical vocabulary (e.g., *forecasted, double-hulled catamaran, flukes*)
• *-ly* endings
• A range of uses for commas
• A range of punctuation (e.g., commas, exclamation point, quotation marks)

Review

The students...

• Discussed the key features of memoir and found places in their piece where these features were included
• Identified the many adverbs in their piece
• Talked about the technical terms they included and how these words strengthened their piece

Extend

Students painted images from their trip and incorporated fun facts about whales. The paintings, the fun facts, and the piece were displayed together in their classroom. Students also wrote their own personal memoir of the trip.

Frequency and Duration

The Prewrite began as students journaled about their experience the evening after the trip. Brainstorming was done the next day using their journals to prompt ideas. The text was then written over three days. Lessons lasted 30 minutes.

<Scene begins with Roxanne exploring a book about Magellan in her classroom.>

Roxanne (R): This is a great book about Magellan. Oooo, look there's a picture of Magellan on his ship! Let me take a closer look.

<Time machine sounds begin. Then you hear the sound of crashing waves. Roxanne is transported back in time. She appears on Magellan's ship.>

R: Where am I? Whoa! There's Ferdinand Magellan himself. I'm gonna go ask him some questions.

R: <Roxanne pauses then yells out.> Sir! Sir! Captain Magellan!

Magellan (M): <Yelling back> Who are you?!!! Why are you on my ship?!!

R: I'm Roxanne. I only wanted to ask you some questions.

M: And then you leave.

R: Yes Captain Magellan. When and where were you born?

M: I was born in Portugal in 1840. My parents died when I was 10.

R: Oh, I'm sorry. What happened to you then?

M: I was made to work as a page for a long time for Queen Leonor of Portugal. When I got older, I wanted to explore so I could find a way to reach the Spice Islands without having to sail around the Cape of Good Hope.

R: What motivated you to go on this journey?

M: I wanted to bring back spices to Portugal and become rich.

Experience

The students were studying world explorers during a social studies unit. As a class, they researched Ferdinand Magellan. Students then worked in pairs to research their own explorer.

Prewrite

This piece aligned with the school's social studies and ELA curriculum expectations. The students recorded their research on a graphic organizer that provided space for different categories of information (e.g., "Motivation for Explorations," "Major Voyages/Journeys," "Discoveries," "Contact With Indigenous People"). Their final project was for the pairs of students to prepare an interview in which one student interviewed the other who acted as the explorer. They were expected to include the information from their research. During Prewrite, the teacher explained how they would need to write an interview in the format of a script. As a class, they would practice this hybrid genre (script/interview/informational text) using Magellan, the explorer with whom all students were familiar.

Compose

The mixed genre (script and historical writing) required the students learn and discuss:
• How to begin with a friendly discussion
• How to write strong and interesting interview questions
• How to include important biographical information in the explorer's answers

(continued)

Note: It was not necessary for the students to write a complete interview for Magellan, as they were expected to do this for their own explorer. After writing several questions and answers, the teacher felt the students understood how to compose this type of text and were ready to do it on their own.

Share the Pen
They focused on:
• Format and layout needed when writing a script
• Spelling and punctuation were addressed as needed

Review
The students...
• Discussed the features of script writing
• Identified the strong/interesting interview questions
• Identified the format, layout, and font issues that were practiced

Extend
The students worked in pairs to write their own interview/scripts. They recorded their interview on GarageBand, with one student reading the part of the questioner and the other reading the explorer. Sound effects were included if desired. The students shared their recordings with parents at student-led conferences.

Frequency and Duration
The students worked on the Prewrite (collecting research on Magellan) in one lesson. They wrote the script in a lesson several days later, after they had completed the research on their own explorers. The interactive writing lesson for this script was one 30-minute session.

Rocking the Rock Cycle

The three types of rocks that make up Earth's crust are sedimentary, igneous, and metamorphic rocks. The Rock Cycle forms these rocks which come in diverse shapes, colors, and sizes. Sedimentary rocks are formed when sediments such as weathered rocks, sand, and dead organisms experience forceful pressure and are cemented into layers. Sedimentary rocks transform into metamorphic rock when the rock encounters extreme heat and pressure. Igneous rocks are created when magma, or molten rock, cools and solidifies. A process that morphs igneous rocks into sediment is called weathering and erosion. Igneous rocks can mutate into metamorphic rocks when they undergo a great amount of heat and pressure. Metamorphic rocks are created from igneous and sedimentary rocks that have been exposed to an extravagant amount of heat and pressure. The melting process alters metamorphic rocks by changing them into magma, while weathering and erosion deconstruct metamorphic rocks into sediment. The Rock Cycle includes numerous processes that form and modify Earth's crust.

Experience

The students were studying rocks as part of their fifth-grade science curriculum. In addition, students were preparing for their annual standardized science assessment.

Prewrite

This piece aligned with the state's expectations for science writing. The students prepared to respond to an extended response question that would mirror their standardized science test. The prompt was: "Explain how the three kinds of rock that make up the Earth's crust form. In your explanation be sure to include the names of the three kinds of rock, the processes that form each kind of rock, and the processes that change each kind of rock." They planned for their writing by reviewing their previous written notes and graphic organizers on the three kinds of rock and the rock cycle processes. Further, they discussed the importance of including a clear topic sentence, key details, and a strong ending.

Compose

For each sentence, the teacher guided students to use their notes to inform their ideas and to include precise vocabulary (e.g., *weathered*, *cemented*, *deconstruct*). Ahead of time, the teacher planned that the organization of the paragraph would be to begin with a general topic sentence, followed by detailed sentences about each of the three types of rocks. In each case, she supported students to first define the type of rock and then to build an additional sentence that explains its role in the rock cycle. Of particular interest was the teacher's expectation that students avoid the word *change*. She paused frequently when they used that word to see if they could come up with other verbs (e.g., *transform*, *morph*, *alter*). At several points, when students shared different ideas, the teacher combined them in order to model how to compose complex sentences. This collaborative effort allowed students to discuss and practice how to expand their ideas in order to write a more sophisticated sentence.

(continued)

Share the Keyboard

They focused on:

- Spelling of technical terms (e.g., *sedimentary*, *igneous*, *erosion*)
- Using a comma for a list and to signal a point of clarification (e.g., "when magma, or molten rock, cools and solidifies.")
- Keyboarding/typing skills (e.g., using the tab key, capitalization, word spacing)

Review

The teacher highlighted...

- The many examples of precise vocabulary and strong verbs
- The overall organization of the piece (e.g., the topic sentence, details about each type of rock, a concluding sentence at the end)
- Places where ideas were combined to form a complex (and more interesting) sentence

Extend

The teacher printed and copied the piece for students to keep in their science folders. They used the piece as an example of how to answer an extended response question effectively on a standardized assessment.

Frequency and Duration

This piece was completed over three 30-minute lessons. After each sentence was composed, students were selected to type it onto a Word document that was projected onto a screen for everyone to see.

Universal Principles of Interactive Writing: Five Ideas That Hold for All Grades

You have walked carefully through each step of an interactive writing lesson and thought about how to pull it all together. Now you are ready to begin! Clearly, there are modifications and adjustments to be made as writers mature. However, we end by highlighting five universal principles that hold for interactive writing across all grades: (1) Value each step in the lesson, (2) Balance the planned and unplanned teaching opportunities, (3) Make intentional teaching decisions as writers develop, (4) Make explicit links between a whole-class lesson and students' own writing, and (5) Foster a classroom environment that offers a place for "safe practice."

Value Each Step in the Lesson

Research suggests that good literacy teaching is instructionally dense so that a single lesson includes multiple goals (Wharton-McDonald, Pressley, & Hampston, 1998). Interactive writing exemplifies this principle as each lesson component (i.e., Experience, Prewrite, Compose, Share the Pen, Review, and Extend) plays an essential role in offering myriad teaching opportunities. In each chapter that focuses on an individual step in the lesson (3–8), we provided a rationale for the merits of that step.

By now you know that in the composing phase of a lesson, you and your students work together to negotiate the message you will write. During this process, you develop students' writing *craft*, including ideas, organization, sentence fluency, word choice, and voice. When you share the pen or keyboard with students to construct the message, you focus on *conventions* of writing, including spelling, punctuation, grammar, handwriting, and text layout. Review is a unique opportunity to highlight key teaching points about both craft and conventions in an interactive way around a piece all students have created. This brief but important step brings closure to an interactive writing session and helps ensure that students connect the group work with their own independent writing. Extend offers rich opportunities to present your work and connect with other areas of the literacy curriculum.

The numerous opportunities for instruction about craft and conventions as well as about the many nuances of the writing process can be met only when each step of the lesson is planned carefully and implemented. Thus, we strongly recommend that you avoid eliminating any of the steps in interactive writing as that would then eliminate valuable and unique learning opportunities.

Balance the Planned and Unplanned Teaching Opportunities

A well-planned interactive writing lesson considers where student writers are and what writing skills or strategies are most needed to propel them further. The lesson planning occurs before the interactive writing session and is informed by both student data (both formal and informal writing samples) and by your unit or grade-level plans. During the interactive lesson, however, there are always unplanned instructional opportunities. The most effective teachers seize these opportunities and use them to lift the instruction to a new and higher level.

You might have planned the instruction around a particular genre and thought ahead about key principles to highlight. You facilitate the conversation carefully with students during Prewrite and Compose so that the key writing principles are included. That said, there will *always* be spontaneous and organic aspects of this experience that will be unique and genuine to the interaction. One never knows in advance the exact wording students will choose for their text. Therefore, you can never anticipate fully the conventions and specific aspects of craft that will be relevant to teach.

Finding the balance between thoughtful planning and organic teaching can be challenging. However, you can master this skill as you and the students become more experienced with the method. As a result, you will maximize the potential learning opportunities for students. The overarching goal of interactive writing is to teach students strategies about writing that they can use themselves. The skillful balancing of planning ahead and teaching in the moment allows you to achieve this goal.

Make Intentional Teaching Decisions as Writers Develop

Although interactive writing offers a clear structure for a lesson, following this structure alone does not guarantee student learning. Moreover, thoughtful interactive writing instruction does not mean having the students write every letter of every word or attending to every learning opportunity that arises. The real power comes from instructional decision-making relating to the unique strengths and needs of your students at a particular moment in time. The most effective teachers make strategic decisions about each child scribe and are very intentional about each teaching point in order to maximize student learning (Roth, 2009).

The roots of these instructional decisions, which fuel an efficient and effective lesson, come from teacher analysis of formal and informal assessments of students' literacy skills. Use this data to select the most appropriate writing skills and strategies for *your* students. Thus, the lessons are matched to students' needs rather than a concept that may have already been mastered or one that is too hard.

Simultaneously, you adjust your interactive writing instruction thoughtfully over the course of the year and across the grades as your students develop as readers and writers. You create a developmentally appropriate gradient of text for students by starting more simply in the fall, making adjustments throughout the year based on data, and, ultimately, becoming more sophisticated by the spring.

A universal principle for interactive writing in all grades is the value placed on thoughtful teacher decisions. Every lesson provides multiple opportunities for direct instruction about language conventions, concepts about print, types of writing, and traits of writing in a meaningful context. However, because there are so many opportunities for teaching throughout the lesson, you must be thoughtful about how you focus students' attention on the basis of what they need to learn.

Make Explicit Links to Students' Own Writing

The ultimate goal of interactive writing is to improve students' independent writing. In interactive writing, you are authoring *with* students to guide and support them in how to do it alone. Teachers who are most effective with this method are deliberate in their talk with students about how to apply what they are learning during whole-class interactive writing lessons to their independent writing (Roth, 2009). Some students will make these connections independently, while others need explicit direction.

For example, you might say, "The way we put commas between words in the list we wrote today is what you always need to do in your own writing" or "The way we took our two ideas and combined them into one longer and more interesting sentence is something good writers do. When you write on your own, remember to do this too." This explicit link to students' independent writing needs to happen in every interactive writing lesson. Using clear language will help students consolidate what they have learned and understand how to improve their own work.

Foster a Classroom Environment That Offers a Place for "Safe Practice"

Throughout interactive writing, students are encouraged to talk with their peers about their ideas and experiences. This opportunity to engage in rich collaborative discussions throughout the writing process is helpful for all students (Fisher & Frey, 2010; Wasik & Iannone-Campbell, 2012). It is particularly powerful for struggling writers and ELs who may be reluctant to speak in more formal situations (Gibbons, 2015; Hill & Flynn, 2006; Mason & Galloway, 2012). The congenial energy of the Compose conversations eliminates any fears about "saying it wrong" or "not making sense." Rather, it is the *perfect* time for students to take risks with sentence composing as they try out new words, phrases, and sentences. As they take these risks, it is imperative that you honor their attempt rather than correct or dismiss it.

It is also important for you to resist that urge to have students select the word in *your* mind. There may likely be moments during Compose when you know that there is a better or more appropriate word to use. Rather than have students try to "guess" the word in your head, simply provide it for them. This scaffolded support allows your writers to hear and learn new vocabulary. This is the essence of the back-and-forth collaboration between you and the students.

Consider the following example: As fifth graders composed a sentence during science, Melissa hoped they would come up with the word *inform* rather than the overused word *tell*. When she asked students if there was another word that might work, the students could not come up with anything that fit. In that moment, we recommend that you offer up the word *inform*—in fact, we believe this is *the* moment to *teach* students about how and why that word is a better option.

Similarly, Share the Pen must always be a supportive rather than punitive experience for students. When a student makes a mistake, you follow with a friendly response such as, "Let me grab the tape, and we can fix it." Or, if Collins makes an error, it is not time for Annabel to fix it. Rather, cover the error with the tape, and *Collins* gets to do it again. And succeed. The bottom line is that throughout every phase of the lesson, you promote and encourage risk-taking. You are the guide who supports students in trying new things and being successful.

Final Thoughts

An interactive writing lesson done well is cohesive and comprehensive. In these one-page summaries, we highlight what teachers focused on at every phase of the writing. As we have said before, the finished products are valuable. However, the interactive writing *process* is most important to understand and remember. The progression of writing development is striking as we look at the PreK–5 gradient of text.

At the same time, these lessons are united by five principles that hold throughout all the grades. In every lesson, the teachers valued each step along the way, balanced the planned and unplanned opportunities, made intentional decisions, linked explicitly the collaborative writing back to their students' own writing, and, throughout the lesson, fostered a classroom environment that offered a place for "safe practice." With these ideas pulled together, we hope you are now ready to begin or refine your own implementation of interactive writing!

CONCLUSION

We set out to write a straightforward "how-to" book about interactive writing—a *small* instructional practice that yields *big* results for students and for you. Our goal was to introduce you to this instructionally rich and efficient method of writing instruction through words, pictures, and teachers' voices. We began by showing you finished interactive writing pieces and then slowly and systematically unpacked and described the details that are crucial to knowing and understanding the value of interactive writing. Later, we stepped back and thought about what it means to launch this practice in classrooms in regard to classroom management and teacher planning. We then highlighted and described one last time how the method comes together to form a cohesive lesson, wrapping up with several universal principles that hold across all grade levels.

We envision this book as your guide or manual, offering both concrete suggestions and some high-level conceptual understanding of how and why to implement interactive writing. As we share our closing thoughts, we offer once more the compelling ideas that make interactive writing a practice worthy of your full attention.

Interactive writing is a* small *method of instruction meant to complement and support other approaches to teaching writing. It is a singular, straightforward practice that stands alone as a method to master. Interactive writing is relatively easy to implement in that it is cost-effective; minimal materials are needed. It is also time-effective. For lower grades, the daily lessons are short in duration. In the upper grades, the actual lesson may be longer in order to meet the complexity of the writing; however, the frequency of lessons decreases. In addition, the predictable nature and sequence grounds the method and makes it doable for busy teachers.

Although it is a rich and effective method, interactive writing is not meant to be used in isolation. Every lesson connects and integrates other relevant areas of your literacy curriculum, including reading, spelling, grammar, and vocabulary. As a method of instruction, interactive writing is nested within the gradual release of responsibility model between teacher modeling and shared writing on one side and independent writing on the other side.

For us, it represents the best form of guided writing instruction, as it is driven by what your students need and what scaffolds you, as the teacher, can offer them as they make their journey toward independence. When used regularly along with teacher-directed, shared, and independent writing, interactive writing ensures that your students have experienced an opportunity to write *with teacher support.*

Interactive writing is genuine and flexible. Every interactive writing lesson centers on a meaningful topic as well as a real purpose and audience for writing. Although your preparation is thoughtful *and* there is a clear structure to each interactive writing session, every lesson evolves organically as you and your students bring your authentic understandings of a shared experience to the lesson.

Interactive writing includes both planned and unplanned moments. You can never predict what a student might say during any phase of a lesson. This method allows and encourages you to seize and maximize these unplanned opportunities when they offer a teachable moment that will advance and strengthen the writing and, more important, the writers. The lessons are flexible in that you adjust your teaching points when needed to meet students' differentiated needs.

In addition, interactive writing is an approach that can be used across all content areas and can work with all kinds of curriculum. It can be delivered through both whole-group and small-group structures. This flexibility allows you to teach your students where they are as writers and offer them genuine instructional guidance that is both timely and relevant.

Interactive writing attends to both the craft and conventions of writing. From the very beginning, you know and consider the audience, the purpose, and the organization of the piece (Prewrite). In every lesson you work with your students to develop and refine the ideas, the words, the sentences, and the voice of the writing (Compose). Then, as you move into Share the Pen/ Keyboard, you emphasize the importance of writing conventions as you teach skills such as correct letter formation, spelling, and punctuation. The inclusive nature of this method guarantees that you are teaching writing in its complete and full manner. Young writers need to know all of these elements and, moreover, need to practice them simultaneously in real time, just as real authors do. Interactive writing requires that you do this each and every time! Knowing that you are "covering" all aspects of writing when you use this method is both reassuring and empowering.

Interactive writing promotes collaboration and community. Gathering students together to write about a shared experience naturally leads to collaborative work. However, the benefits of this team approach where everyone has something to offer last far beyond the lesson. As you and your students talk about the ideas and words of your writing, energy and enthusiasm grow between and among students. Students support one another as they build and refine the sentences. Your role requires skillful and positive facilitation to help students feel ownership of the piece as they connect with one another to make the writing theirs.

This community of writers solidifies and strengthens every time you use interactive writing. Each lesson has a moment when you can harness your students' diverse strengths and skills and lift their writing to a higher level. When the writing is finalized and extended in genuine ways, you have created a powerful illustration of the journey you have shared together as writers.

Interactive writing yields big results for students and for you. As you work through the many facets of this method and delve into teaching the writing process in this way, you will have many rich conversations with your students. This experience can help crystalize *your* understanding of good writing and instruction. At the same time, it can advance your students' independent writing, which is the ultimate goal. Their understanding of how writers plan, draft, revise, edit, and publish is strengthened.

Every lesson also is packed with multiple literacy learning opportunities beyond the craft and conventions of writing. Students practice important foundational skills as they articulate the words and phrases of the writing. They work on speaking and listening as they discuss their ideas for a text and negotiate the precise words to be written. And, as they read and reread their writing, they practice oral reading and fluency. Finally, after actively participating to complete interactive writing pieces, students see themselves as writers. With this mind-set in place, students approach the next writing task more skillfully and more confidently. Interactive writing yields many *big* results and deserves prioritized attention as we strive to teach our students to write with authority, credibility, conviction, and passion.

REFERENCES

Bangert-Drowns, R.L. (1993). The word processor as an instructional tool: A meta-analysis of word processing in writing instruction. *Review of Educational Research, 63*(1), 69–93. doi:10.3102/00346543063001069

Bloodgood, J.W. (1999). What's in a name? Children's name writing and literacy acquisition. *Reading Research Quarterly, 34*(3), 342–367. doi:10.1598/RRQ.34.3.5

Bromley, K. (2011). Best practices in teaching writing. In L.M. Morrow & L.B. Gambrell (Eds.), *Best practices in literacy instruction* (4th ed., pp. 295–318). New York, NY: Guilford.

Brotherton, S., & Williams, C. (2002). Interactive writing instruction in a first-grade Title I literacy program. *Journal of Reading Education, 27*(3), 8–19.

Brozo, W. (2003). Literary license. *Voices From the Middle, 10*(3), 43–45.

Button, K., Johnson, M., & Furgerson, P. (1996). Interactive writing in a primary grade classroom. *The Reading Teacher, 49*(6), 446–454.

Callella, T., & Jordano, K. (2000). *Interactive writing: Students and teachers "sharing the pen" to create meaningful text*. Huntington Beach, CA: Creative Teaching.

Clay, M.M. (1975). *What did I write? Beginning writing behaviour*. Auckland, New Zealand: Heinemann.

Clay, M.M. (1991). *Becoming literate: The construction of inner control*. Portsmouth, NH: Heinemann.

Coker, D., Jr. (2013). Writing instruction in preschool and kindergarten. In S. Graham, C.A. MacArthur, & J. Fitzgerald (Eds.), *Best practices in writing instruction* (2nd ed., pp. 26–47). New York, NY: Guilford.

Culham, R. (2003). *6 + 1 traits of writing: The complete guide, grades 3 and up*. New York, NY: Scholastic.

Culham, R. (2005). *6 + 1 traits of writing: The complete guide for the primary grades*. New York, NY: Scholastic.

Cunningham, P.M. (2011). Best practices in teaching phonological awareness and phonics. In L.M. Morrow & L.B. Gambrell (Eds.), *Best practices in literacy instruction* (4th ed., pp. 199–233). New York, NY: Guilford.

Darling-Hammond, L., & Austin, K. (2003). *11: Lessons for life—learning and transfer* [The Learning Classroom: Theory Into Practice session overview]. Retrieved from www.learner.org/courses/learningclassroom/session_overviews/learn_transfer_home11.html

Fisher, D., & Frey, N. (2007a). *Checking for understanding: Formative assessment techniques for your classroom*. Alexandria, VA: Association for Supervision and Curriculum Development.

Fisher, D., & Frey, N. (2007b). *Scaffolded writing instruction: Teaching with a gradual-release framework*. New York, NY: Scholastic.

Fisher, D., & Frey, N. (2010). Structuring the talk: Ensuring academic conversations matter. *The Clearing House, 84*(1), 15–20.

Fisher, D., & Frey, N. (2013). A range of writing across the content areas. *The Reading Teacher, 67*(2), 96–101.

Ganske, K. (Ed.). (2014). Write now! Empowering writers in today's K–6 classroom. Newark, DE: International Reading Association.

Gibbons, P. (2015). *Scaffolding language, scaffolding learning: Teaching English language learners in the mainstream classroom* (2nd ed.). Portsmouth, NH: Heinemann.

Gilbert, J., & Graham, S. (2010). Teaching writing to elementary students in grades 4–6: A national survey. *The Elementary School Journal, 110*(4), 494–518. doi:10.1086/651193

Goldberg, A., Russell, M., & Cook, A. (2003). The effect of computers on student writing: A meta-analysis of studies from 1992–2002. *The Journal of Technology, Learning, and Assessment, 2*(1), 3–51.

Graham, S., & Harris, K.R. (2013). Designing an effective writing program. In S. Graham, C.A. MacArthur, & J. Fitzgerald (Eds.), *Best practices in writing instruction* (2nd ed., pp. 3–25). New York, NY: Guilford.

Graham, S., & Harris, K.R. (2014). Six recommendations for teaching writing to meet the Common Core. In K. Ganske (Ed.), *Write now! Empowering writers in today's K–6 classroom* (pp. 18–33). Newark, DE: International Reading Association. doi:10.1598/0353.02

Graham, S., Harris, K.R., & Hebert, M.A. (2011). It is more than just the message: Presentation effects in scoring writing. *Focus on Exceptional Children, 44*(4), 1–12.

Graham, S., & Hebert, M.A. (2010). *Writing to read: Evidence for how writing can improve reading.* Washington, DC: Alliance for Excellent Education.

Graham, S., MacArthur, C.A., & Fitzgerald, J. (Eds.). (2013). *Best practices in writing instruction* (2nd ed.). New York, NY: Guilford.

Graham, S., & Perin, D. (2007a). A meta-analysis of writing instruction for adolescent students. *Journal of Educational Psychology, 99*(3), 445–476. doi:10.1037/0022-0663.99.3.445

Graham, S., & Perin, D. (2007b). *Writing next: Effective strategies to improve writing of adolescents in middle and high schools.* Washington, DC: Alliance for Excellent Education.

Hayes, J.R. (1996). A new framework for understanding cognition and affect in writing. In C.M. Levy & S. Ransdell (Eds.), *The science of writing: Theories, methods, individual differences, and applications* (pp. 1–28). Mahwah, NJ: Erlbaum.

Hill, J., & Flynn, K. (2006). *Classroom instruction that works with English language learners.* Alexandria, VA: Association for Supervision and Curriculum Development.

Hunter, M. (1982). *Mastery teaching.* Thousand Oaks, CA: Corwin.

Jago, C. (2014). Growing writers: Teaching argumentative writing through evidence-based thinking. In K. Ganske (Ed.), *Write now! Empowering writers in today's K–6 classroom* (pp. 72–86). Newark, DE: International Reading Association. doi:10.1598/0353.05

Jones, F., & Jones, P. (2013). *Tools for teaching: Discipline, instruction, and motivation* (3rd ed.). Santa Cruz, CA: Frederick H. Jones.

Juel, C. (1988). Learning to read and write: A longitudinal study of 54 children from first through fourth grade. *Journal of Educational Psychology, 80*(4), 437–447. doi:10.1037/0022-0663.80.4.437

Kuhn, M.R., & Rasinski, T. (2011). Best practices in fluency instruction. In L.M. Morrow & L.B. Gambrell (Eds.), *Best practices in literacy instruction* (4th ed., pp. 276–294). New York, NY: Guilford.

Lee, J., Grigg, W., & Donahue, P. (2007). *The Nation's Report Card: Reading 2007* (NCES 2007-496). Washington, DC: National Center for Education Statistics, Institute of Education Sciences, U.S. Department of Education.

Lemov, D. (2014). *Teach like a champion 2.0: 62 techniques that put students on the path to college.* San Francisco, CA: Jossey-Bass.

Marzano, R. (2007). *The art and science of teaching: A comprehensive framework for effective instruction.* Alexandria, VA: Association for Supervision and Curriculum Development.

Marzano, R., Marzano, J., & Pickering, D. (2003). *Classroom instruction that works: Research-based strategies for every teacher.* Alexandria, VA: Association for Supervision and Curriculum Development.

Mason, P., & Galloway, E. (2012). Let them talk! *Reading Today, 29*(4), 29–30.

McCarrier, A., Pinnell, G.S., & Fountas, I.C. (2000). *Interactive writing: How language and literacy come together, K–2.* Portsmouth, NH: Heinemann.

Mermelstein, L. (2013). *Self-directed writers: The third essential element in the writing workshop.* Portsmouth, NH: Heinemann.

Morphy, P., & Graham, S. (2012). Word processing programs and weaker writers/readers: A meta-analysis of research findings. *Reading and Writing, 25*(3), 641–678. doi:10.1007/s11145-010-9292-5

Morrow, L.M., Tracey, D.H., & Del Nero, J.R. (2011). Best practices in early literacy: Preschool, kindergarten, and first grade. In L.M. Morrow & L.B. Gambrell (Eds.), *Best practices in literacy instruction* (4th ed., pp. 67–95). New York, NY: Guilford.

National Center for Education Statistics. (2012). *The Nation's Report Card: Writing 2011* (NCES 2012-470). Washington, DC: National Center for Education Statistics, Institute of Education Sciences, U.S. Department of Education.

National Commission on Writing in America's Schools and Colleges. (2003). *The neglected "R": The need for a writing revolution.* New York, NY: College Board.

National Governors Association Center for Best Practices & Council of Chief State School Officers. (2010). *Common Core State Standards for English language arts and literacy in history/social studies, science, and technical subjects.* Washington, DC: Authors.

Nolen, S. (2007). The role of literate communities in the development of children's interest in writing. In S. Hidi & P. Boscolo (Eds.), *Writing and motivation* (pp. 241–355). Oxford, England: Elsevier.

Pearson, P.D., & Gallagher, M.C. (1983). The instruction of reading comprehension. *Contemporary Educational Psychology, 8*(3), 317–344. doi:10.1016/0361-476X(83)90019-X

Phelan, T., & Schonour, S. (2004). *1, 2, 3, magic for teachers: Effective classroom discipline pre-K through grade 8.* Glen Ellyn, IL: Parentmagic.

Pinnell, G.S., & Fountas, I.C. (1998). *Word matters: Teaching phonics and spelling in the reading/writing classroom.* Portsmouth, NH: Heinemann.

Pinnell, G.S., & Fountas, I.C. (2011). *The continuum of literacy learning grades preK–8: A guide to teaching.* Portsmouth, NH: Heinemann.

Popham, W.J. (2008). *Transformative assessment.* Alexandria, VA: Association for Supervision and Curriculum Development.

Reutzel, D.R. (2011). Organizing effective literacy instruction: Differentiating instruction to meet student needs. In L.M. Morrow & L.B. Gambrell (Eds.), *Best practices in literacy instruction* (4th ed., pp. 412–435). New York, NY: Guilford.

Rideout, V.J., Foehr, U.G., & Roberts, D.F. (2010). *Generation M²: Media in the lives of 8- to 18-year-olds.* Menlo Park, CA: Kaiser Family Foundation.

Roth, K. (2009). *Interactive writing: Investigating the effectiveness of a dynamic approach to writing instruction for first graders* (Unpublished doctoral dissertation). Harvard Graduate School of Education, Cambridge, MA.

Roth, K., & Dabrowski, J. (2014). Extending interactive writing into grades 2–5. *The Reading Teacher, 68*(1), 33–44. doi:10.1002/trtr.1270

Roth, K., & Guinee, K. (2011). Ten minutes a day: The impact of interactive writing instruction on first graders' independent writing. *Journal of Early Childhood Literacy, 11*(3), 331–361. doi:10.1177/1468798411409300

Saddler, B. (2013). Best practices in sentence construction skills. In S. Graham, C.A. MacArthur, & J. Fitzgerald (Eds.), *Best practices in writing instruction* (2nd ed., pp. 238–256). New York, NY: Guilford.

Saphier, J., Haley-Speca, M., & Gower, R. (2008). *The skillful teacher: Building your teaching skills* (6th ed.). Acton, MA: Research for Better Teaching.

Schlagal, B. (2013). Best practices in spelling and handwriting. In S. Graham, C.A. MacArthur, & J. Fitzgerald (Eds.), *Best practices in writing instruction* (2nd ed., pp. 257–283). New York, NY: Guilford.

Schmoker, M. (2011). *Focus: Elevating the essentials to radically improve student learning.* Alexandria, VA: Association for Supervision and Curriculum Development.

Shanahan, T. (2014). Writing about reading: Writing instruction in the age of the Common Core State Standards. In K. Ganske (Ed.), *Write now! Empowering writers in today's K–6 classroom* (pp. 3–17). Newark, DE: International Reading Association. doi:10.1598/0353.01

Spandel, V. (2013). *Creating writers: 6 traits, process, workshop, and literature* (6th ed.). Boston, MA: Pearson.

Swartz, S.L., Klein, A.F., & Shook, R.E. (2001). *Interactive writing and interactive editing: Making connections between writing and reading.* Parsippany, NJ: Dominie.

Tompkins, G.E., & Collom, S. (2004). *Sharing the pen: Interactive writing with young children.* Parsippany, NJ: Pearson.

Vygotsky, L. (1978). *Mind in society: The development of higher psychological processes* (M. Cole, V. John-Steiner, S. Scribner, & E. Souberman, Eds. & Trans.). Cambridge, MA: Harvard University Press.

Wall, H. (2008). Interactive writing beyond the primary grades. *The Reading Teacher, 62*(2), 149–152. doi:10.1598/RT.62.2.6

Wasik, B., & Iannone-Campbell, C. (2012). Developing vocabulary through purposeful, strategic conversations. *The Reading Teacher, 66*(4), 321–332. doi:10.1002/TRTR.01095

Wharton-McDonald, R., Pressley, M., & Hampston, J. (1998). Literacy instruction in nine first-grade classrooms: Teacher characteristics and student achievement. *The Elementary School Journal, 99*(2), 101–128. doi:10.1086/461918

Williams, C., Sherry, T., Robinson, N., & Hungler, D. (2012). The practice page as mediational tool for interactive writing instruction. *The Reading Teacher, 65*(5), 330–340. doi:10.1002/TRTR.01051

Wolfe, P. (2011). Neuroscience reaffirms Madeline Hunter's model. *ASCD Express, 6*(8). Retrieved from www.ascd.org/ascd-express/vol6/608-wolfe.aspx

Wong, H., Wong, R., Jondahl, S., & Ferguson, O. (2014). *The classroom management book.* Mountain View, CA: Harry K. Wong.

Yancey, K.B. (2009). *Writing in the 21st century: A report from the National Council of Teachers of English.* Urbana, IL: National Council of Teachers of English.

LITERATURE CITED

Babbit, N. (1975). *Tuck everlasting.* New York, NY: Farrar, Straus and Giroux.

Beeler, S. (1998). *Throw your tooth on the roof: Tooth traditions from around the world.* Boston, MA: Houghton Mifflin.

Curtis, C.P. (1999). *Bud, not Buddy.* New York, NY: Random House.

Lin, G. (2009). *Where the mountain meets the moon.* New York, NY: Little, Brown.

Scieszka, J. (1989). *The true story of the 3 little pigs!* New York, NY: Viking.

Wulffson, D. (2000). *Toys! Amazing stories behind some great inventions.* New York, NY: Henry Holt.